50 Mexican Magic Recipes for Home

By: Kelly Johnson

Table of Contents

- Beef Tacos
- Chicken Enchiladas
- Beef Burritos
- Chicken Fajitas
- Cheese Quesadillas
- Shrimp Tacos
- Pork Carnitas
- Chicken Tortilla Soup
- Beef Chili
- Chiles Rellenos
- Beef Empanadas
- Chicken Mole
- Fish Tacos
- Beef Tamales
- Chicken Tinga
- Carne Asada
- Beef Chimichangas
- Salsa Verde
- Guacamole
- Pico de Gallo
- Mexican Rice
- Refried Beans
- Chile Con Carne
- Chipotle Chicken
- Shrimp Ceviche
- Chilaquiles
- Chicken Pozole
- Birria
- Huevos Rancheros
- Tostadas
- Sopa de Lima
- Tamales de Elote
- Beef Barbacoa
- Mexican Street Corn (Elote)
- Enchiladas Suizas

- Carnitas Tacos
- Barbacoa Tacos
- Al Pastor Tacos
- Pozole Rojo
- Flan
- Churros
- Sopapillas
- Tres Leches Cake
- Mexican Wedding Cookies
- Margaritas
- Horchata
- Micheladas
- Agua Fresca
- Paloma
- Mexican Hot Chocolate

Beef Tacos

Ingredients:

For the beef filling:

- 500g (1 lb) ground beef
- 1 tablespoon olive oil
- 1 onion, finely chopped
- 2 cloves garlic, minced
- 1 tablespoon chili powder
- 1 teaspoon ground cumin
- 1/2 teaspoon paprika
- 1/2 teaspoon dried oregano
- Salt and pepper to taste
- 1/4 cup tomato sauce
- 1/4 cup beef broth or water
- Juice of 1 lime (optional)

For serving:

- 8-10 small corn or flour tortillas
- Shredded lettuce
- Diced tomatoes
- Diced onions
- Sliced jalapeños
- Shredded cheese (such as cheddar or Monterey Jack)
- Sour cream
- Salsa
- Chopped cilantro
- Lime wedges

Instructions:

1. Heat the olive oil in a large skillet over medium heat. Add the chopped onion and cook until softened, about 5 minutes.
2. Add the minced garlic to the skillet and cook for another minute, until fragrant.
3. Add the ground beef to the skillet, breaking it up with a spoon. Cook the beef, stirring occasionally, until browned and cooked through, about 6-8 minutes.
4. Once the beef is browned, add the chili powder, ground cumin, paprika, dried oregano, salt, and pepper to the skillet. Stir to coat the beef in the spices.
5. Pour in the tomato sauce and beef broth or water. Stir to combine and simmer the beef mixture for 5-10 minutes, allowing the flavors to meld. If desired, squeeze in the juice of 1 lime for extra freshness.
6. While the beef is simmering, warm the tortillas. You can heat them in a dry skillet over medium heat for about 30 seconds on each side or wrap them in foil and warm them in a preheated oven at 180°C (350°F) for 5-10 minutes.
7. Once the beef filling is ready, assemble the tacos. Place a spoonful of the beef filling onto each tortilla, then top with shredded lettuce, diced tomatoes, diced onions, sliced jalapeños, shredded cheese, sour cream, salsa, chopped cilantro, and a squeeze of lime juice.
8. Serve the beef tacos immediately, with additional toppings on the side if desired.

Enjoy your homemade beef tacos, a flavorful and satisfying meal that's perfect for any occasion!

Chicken Enchiladas

Ingredients:

For the chicken filling:

- 2 boneless, skinless chicken breasts (about 500g or 1 lb)
- 1 tablespoon olive oil
- 1 onion, chopped
- 2 cloves garlic, minced
- 1 teaspoon ground cumin
- 1 teaspoon chili powder
- Salt and pepper to taste
- 1 can (400g or 14 oz) diced tomatoes, drained
- 1 can (200g or 7 oz) diced green chilies, drained (optional)
- 1/4 cup chopped fresh cilantro (coriander)

For the enchilada sauce:

- 2 tablespoons olive oil
- 2 tablespoons all-purpose flour
- 2 tablespoons chili powder
- 1 teaspoon ground cumin
- 1/2 teaspoon garlic powder
- 1/4 teaspoon dried oregano
- 2 cups chicken broth
- Salt and pepper to taste

For assembling:

- 8-10 corn or flour tortillas
- 1 cup shredded cheese (such as cheddar or Monterey Jack)
- Chopped fresh cilantro (coriander) for garnish
- Sour cream, diced tomatoes, sliced jalapeños, avocado slices, and lime wedges for serving (optional)

Instructions:

1. Preheat your oven to 180°C (350°F). Lightly grease a 9x13-inch baking dish.
2. In a large skillet, heat the olive oil over medium heat. Add the chopped onion and cook until softened, about 5 minutes. Add the minced garlic, ground cumin, chili powder, salt, and pepper, and cook for another minute until fragrant.
3. Add the chicken breasts to the skillet and cook until browned on both sides, about 6-8 minutes per side. Remove the chicken from the skillet and let it cool slightly, then shred it using two forks.
4. Return the shredded chicken to the skillet, along with the diced tomatoes, diced green chilies (if using), and chopped cilantro. Stir to combine and cook for another 5 minutes, allowing the flavors to meld. Remove from heat and set aside.
5. To make the enchilada sauce, heat the olive oil in a saucepan over medium heat. Stir in the flour and cook for 1-2 minutes, until lightly browned and fragrant.
6. Stir in the chili powder, ground cumin, garlic powder, and dried oregano. Cook for another minute, then gradually whisk in the chicken broth until smooth.
7. Bring the sauce to a simmer and cook for 5-10 minutes, until thickened. Season with salt and pepper to taste.
8. To assemble the enchiladas, spoon a portion of the chicken filling onto each tortilla, then roll it up tightly and place it seam side down in the prepared baking dish.
9. Pour the enchilada sauce over the rolled tortillas, making sure they are evenly coated.
10. Sprinkle the shredded cheese over the top of the enchiladas.
11. Bake the enchiladas in the preheated oven for 20-25 minutes, until the cheese is melted and bubbly.
12. Remove the enchiladas from the oven and let them cool slightly before serving.
13. Garnish the enchiladas with chopped fresh cilantro and serve with sour cream, diced tomatoes, sliced jalapeños, avocado slices, and lime wedges on the side, if desired.

Enjoy your homemade chicken enchiladas, a flavorful and satisfying meal that's sure to be a hit with your family and friends!

Beef Burritos

Ingredients:

For the beef filling:

- 500g (1 lb) ground beef
- 1 tablespoon olive oil
- 1 onion, finely chopped
- 2 cloves garlic, minced
- 1 bell pepper, diced
- 1 tablespoon chili powder
- 1 teaspoon ground cumin
- 1/2 teaspoon paprika
- Salt and pepper to taste
- 1 can (400g or 14 oz) diced tomatoes, drained
- 1 can (400g or 14 oz) black beans, drained and rinsed
- 1/4 cup chopped fresh cilantro (coriander)

For assembling:

- 8-10 large flour tortillas
- Shredded cheese (such as cheddar or Monterey Jack)
- Cooked rice
- Sour cream
- Salsa
- Chopped fresh cilantro (coriander)
- Lime wedges

Instructions:

1. Heat the olive oil in a large skillet over medium heat. Add the chopped onion and diced bell pepper, and cook until softened, about 5 minutes.
2. Add the minced garlic to the skillet and cook for another minute, until fragrant.

3. Add the ground beef to the skillet and cook until browned, breaking it up with a spoon as it cooks.
4. Once the beef is browned, add the chili powder, ground cumin, paprika, salt, and pepper to the skillet. Stir to coat the beef in the spices.
5. Add the diced tomatoes and black beans to the skillet, stirring to combine. Let the mixture simmer for 5-10 minutes, allowing the flavors to meld. Stir in the chopped cilantro.
6. While the beef filling is simmering, warm the flour tortillas in a dry skillet or microwave according to package instructions.
7. To assemble the burritos, spoon a portion of the beef filling onto each tortilla. Top with cooked rice, shredded cheese, sour cream, salsa, and chopped cilantro.
8. Fold the sides of the tortilla over the filling, then roll it up tightly from the bottom to enclose the filling.
9. Serve the beef burritos immediately, with lime wedges on the side for squeezing over the top.

Enjoy your homemade beef burritos, a delicious and customizable meal that's perfect for a quick and easy dinner!

Chicken Fajitas

Ingredients:

For the marinade:

- 500g (1 lb) boneless, skinless chicken breasts, thinly sliced
- 2 tablespoons olive oil
- 2 cloves garlic, minced
- 1 teaspoon chili powder
- 1 teaspoon ground cumin
- 1/2 teaspoon paprika
- Juice of 1 lime
- Salt and pepper to taste

For the fajitas:

- 2 bell peppers (any color), thinly sliced
- 1 onion, thinly sliced
- 2 tablespoons olive oil
- Salt and pepper to taste
- 8-10 small flour tortillas
- Optional toppings: shredded cheese, sour cream, salsa, guacamole, chopped cilantro, lime wedges

Instructions:

1. In a large bowl, whisk together the olive oil, minced garlic, chili powder, ground cumin, paprika, lime juice, salt, and pepper to make the marinade.
2. Add the sliced chicken breasts to the marinade, tossing to coat evenly. Cover the bowl and let the chicken marinate in the refrigerator for at least 30 minutes, or up to 4 hours for maximum flavor.
3. Heat 1 tablespoon of olive oil in a large skillet or grill pan over medium-high heat. Add the sliced bell peppers and onions to the skillet, and cook, stirring occasionally, until they are softened and slightly charred, about 5-7 minutes.

Season with salt and pepper to taste. Remove the cooked peppers and onions from the skillet and set aside.
4. In the same skillet, add the remaining tablespoon of olive oil. Add the marinated chicken slices to the skillet, spreading them out in an even layer. Cook the chicken, stirring occasionally, until it is cooked through and lightly browned, about 6-8 minutes.
5. Once the chicken is cooked, return the cooked peppers and onions to the skillet, tossing to combine with the chicken. Cook for another minute to heat everything through.
6. Warm the flour tortillas in a dry skillet or microwave according to package instructions.
7. To serve, spoon the chicken and vegetable mixture onto each tortilla. Top with your favorite toppings such as shredded cheese, sour cream, salsa, guacamole, chopped cilantro, and a squeeze of lime juice.
8. Roll up the tortillas tightly to enclose the filling, and serve immediately.

Enjoy your homemade chicken fajitas, a delicious and customizable meal that's perfect for a quick and flavorful dinner!

Cheese Quesadillas

Ingredients:

- 4 large flour tortillas
- 2 cups shredded cheese (such as cheddar, Monterey Jack, or a Mexican cheese blend)
- 2 tablespoons butter or olive oil (for cooking)
- Optional toppings: salsa, sour cream, guacamole, chopped cilantro, sliced jalapeños, diced tomatoes

Instructions:

1. Heat a large skillet or griddle over medium heat.
2. Place one flour tortilla on a flat surface. Sprinkle 1/2 cup of shredded cheese evenly over one half of the tortilla, leaving a small border around the edges.
3. Fold the other half of the tortilla over the cheese to create a half-moon shape.
4. Repeat the process with the remaining tortillas and cheese.
5. Once the skillet is hot, add 1/2 tablespoon of butter or olive oil to the skillet. Place one of the filled tortillas in the skillet and cook for 2-3 minutes on each side, or until the tortilla is golden brown and crispy, and the cheese is melted.
6. Remove the cooked quesadilla from the skillet and place it on a cutting board. Repeat the cooking process with the remaining quesadillas.
7. Once all the quesadillas are cooked, use a sharp knife or pizza cutter to slice each quesadilla into wedges or triangles.
8. Serve the cheese quesadillas hot, with your favorite toppings such as salsa, sour cream, guacamole, chopped cilantro, sliced jalapeños, or diced tomatoes on the side for dipping or garnishing.

Enjoy your homemade cheese quesadillas, a simple and delicious dish that's perfect for any occasion!

Shrimp Tacos

Ingredients:

For the shrimp:

- 500g (1 lb) medium shrimp, peeled and deveined
- 2 tablespoons olive oil
- 2 cloves garlic, minced
- 1 teaspoon chili powder
- 1/2 teaspoon ground cumin
- 1/2 teaspoon paprika
- Salt and pepper to taste
- Juice of 1 lime

For assembling:

- 8-10 small flour or corn tortillas
- Shredded cabbage or lettuce
- Diced tomatoes
- Sliced avocado
- Chopped fresh cilantro
- Lime wedges
- Optional toppings: sour cream, salsa, hot sauce

Instructions:

1. In a large bowl, combine the peeled and deveined shrimp with the olive oil, minced garlic, chili powder, ground cumin, paprika, salt, pepper, and lime juice. Toss to coat the shrimp evenly in the marinade. Let the shrimp marinate for 15-30 minutes.
2. While the shrimp is marinating, prepare the toppings for the tacos. Shred the cabbage or lettuce, dice the tomatoes, slice the avocado, chop the fresh cilantro, and cut the lime into wedges.

3. Heat a large skillet or grill pan over medium-high heat. Once hot, add the marinated shrimp to the skillet in a single layer. Cook the shrimp for 2-3 minutes on each side, or until they are pink and opaque.
4. Warm the tortillas in a dry skillet or microwave according to package instructions.
5. To assemble the tacos, place a portion of the cooked shrimp onto each tortilla. Top with shredded cabbage or lettuce, diced tomatoes, sliced avocado, and chopped cilantro.
6. Serve the shrimp tacos hot, with lime wedges on the side for squeezing over the top. Offer optional toppings such as sour cream, salsa, or hot sauce for extra flavor.
7. Enjoy your homemade shrimp tacos, a delicious and satisfying meal that's perfect for any occasion!

Feel free to customize your shrimp tacos with additional toppings or seasonings to suit your taste preferences.

Pork Carnitas

Ingredients:

- 1.5 kg (3.3 lbs) pork shoulder or pork butt, cut into large chunks
- 1 onion, quartered
- 4 cloves garlic, smashed
- 1 orange, quartered
- 2 bay leaves
- 1 teaspoon ground cumin
- 1 teaspoon dried oregano
- 1 teaspoon smoked paprika
- 1 teaspoon chili powder
- Salt and pepper to taste
- 2 tablespoons vegetable oil or lard

Instructions:

1. Preheat your oven to 160°C (325°F).
2. Season the pork chunks generously with salt and pepper.
3. In a large Dutch oven or oven-safe pot, heat the vegetable oil or lard over medium-high heat. Add the seasoned pork chunks to the pot and sear them on all sides until browned, about 5 minutes per side.
4. Once the pork is browned, add the quartered onion, smashed garlic cloves, quartered orange, bay leaves, ground cumin, dried oregano, smoked paprika, and chili powder to the pot. Stir to combine.
5. Pour enough water into the pot to cover the pork by about an inch.
6. Cover the pot with a lid and transfer it to the preheated oven. Let the pork braise in the oven for 2.5 to 3 hours, or until it is tender and easily shreds with a fork.
7. Once the pork is cooked, remove it from the oven and use two forks to shred it into smaller pieces.
8. Heat a large skillet or frying pan over medium-high heat. Transfer the shredded pork carnitas to the skillet, in batches if necessary, and cook them until they are crispy and golden brown on the edges, about 5-7 minutes.
9. Once the carnitas are crispy, remove them from the skillet and drain them on paper towels to remove excess grease.

10. Serve the pork carnitas hot, with your favorite accompaniments such as tortillas, salsa, guacamole, diced onions, chopped cilantro, and lime wedges.

Enjoy your homemade pork carnitas, a delicious and versatile dish that's sure to be a hit with your family and friends!

Chicken Tortilla Soup

Ingredients:

- 2 tablespoons olive oil
- 1 onion, chopped
- 2 cloves garlic, minced
- 1 jalapeño, seeded and diced
- 1 red bell pepper, diced
- 1 carrot, diced
- 1 teaspoon ground cumin
- 1 teaspoon chili powder
- 1/2 teaspoon smoked paprika
- Salt and pepper to taste
- 1 can (400g or 14 oz) diced tomatoes
- 1 can (400g or 14 oz) black beans, drained and rinsed
- 1 can (400g or 14 oz) corn kernels, drained
- 1 liter (4 cups) chicken broth
- 2 cups cooked shredded chicken (from rotisserie or boiled chicken)
- Juice of 1 lime
- Chopped fresh cilantro for garnish
- Tortilla chips for serving
- Optional toppings: shredded cheese, diced avocado, sour cream, sliced jalapeños, lime wedges

Instructions:

1. In a large pot or Dutch oven, heat the olive oil over medium heat. Add the chopped onion, minced garlic, diced jalapeño, diced bell pepper, and diced carrot to the pot. Cook, stirring occasionally, until the vegetables are softened, about 5-7 minutes.
2. Stir in the ground cumin, chili powder, smoked paprika, salt, and pepper, and cook for another minute until fragrant.
3. Add the diced tomatoes (with their juices), black beans, corn kernels, and chicken broth to the pot. Stir to combine.
4. Bring the soup to a simmer, then reduce the heat to low and let it simmer gently for about 15-20 minutes to allow the flavors to meld.

5. Once the soup has simmered for a bit, stir in the cooked shredded chicken and lime juice. Taste and adjust the seasoning with salt and pepper if needed.
6. Continue to cook the soup for another 5-10 minutes until the chicken is heated through.
7. To serve, ladle the chicken tortilla soup into bowls. Top each bowl with chopped fresh cilantro and crushed tortilla chips.
8. Serve the soup hot, with optional toppings such as shredded cheese, diced avocado, sour cream, sliced jalapeños, and lime wedges on the side for garnishing.

Enjoy your homemade chicken tortilla soup, a comforting and flavorful dish that's sure to warm you up from the inside out!

Beef Chili

Ingredients:

- 500g (1 lb) ground beef
- 2 tablespoons olive oil
- 1 onion, chopped
- 3 cloves garlic, minced
- 1 bell pepper, diced
- 2 tablespoons chili powder
- 1 teaspoon ground cumin
- 1/2 teaspoon smoked paprika
- 1/2 teaspoon dried oregano
- 1/4 teaspoon cayenne pepper (optional, for extra heat)
- Salt and pepper to taste
- 1 can (400g or 14 oz) diced tomatoes
- 1 can (400g or 14 oz) kidney beans, drained and rinsed
- 1 cup beef broth
- 1 tablespoon tomato paste
- 1 tablespoon brown sugar (optional, for sweetness)
- Chopped fresh cilantro for garnish (optional)
- Shredded cheese, sour cream, diced onions, and sliced jalapeños for serving (optional)

Instructions:

1. Heat the olive oil in a large pot or Dutch oven over medium heat. Add the chopped onion, minced garlic, and diced bell pepper to the pot. Cook, stirring occasionally, until the vegetables are softened, about 5-7 minutes.
2. Add the ground beef to the pot, breaking it up with a spoon. Cook the beef, stirring occasionally, until browned and cooked through, about 6-8 minutes.
3. Once the beef is browned, stir in the chili powder, ground cumin, smoked paprika, dried oregano, cayenne pepper (if using), salt, and pepper. Cook for another minute until fragrant.
4. Add the diced tomatoes (with their juices), drained and rinsed kidney beans, beef broth, tomato paste, and brown sugar (if using) to the pot. Stir to combine.

5. Bring the chili to a simmer, then reduce the heat to low and let it simmer gently for about 30-45 minutes, stirring occasionally, to allow the flavors to meld and the chili to thicken.
6. Taste the chili and adjust the seasoning with salt and pepper if needed.
7. Once the chili is done, ladle it into bowls and garnish with chopped fresh cilantro if desired.
8. Serve the beef chili hot, with optional toppings such as shredded cheese, sour cream, diced onions, and sliced jalapeños on the side.

Enjoy your homemade beef chili, a hearty and flavorful dish that's perfect for cozy nights in!

Chiles Rellenos

Ingredients:

- 6 large poblano peppers
- 200g (7 oz) queso fresco or Monterey Jack cheese, cut into strips
- 1 cup all-purpose flour
- 4 large eggs, separated
- 1 cup vegetable oil, for frying
- Salt to taste

For the tomato sauce:

- 4 large tomatoes, chopped
- 1 onion, chopped
- 2 cloves garlic, minced
- 1 jalapeño pepper, chopped (optional, for extra heat)
- 1 teaspoon dried oregano
- Salt and pepper to taste

Instructions:

1. Preheat your oven to 200°C (400°F). Place the poblano peppers on a baking sheet and roast them in the oven for 15-20 minutes, or until the skins are blistered and charred. Remove the peppers from the oven and let them cool slightly.
2. Once the peppers are cool enough to handle, carefully peel off the charred skins. Make a slit down the side of each pepper and remove the seeds and membranes, leaving the stems intact.
3. Stuff each pepper with strips of cheese, then close the slits to encase the filling.
4. In a shallow dish, season the flour with salt. In another shallow dish, beat the egg whites until stiff peaks form. In a third shallow dish, lightly beat the egg yolks.
5. Heat the vegetable oil in a large skillet over medium heat.
6. Roll each stuffed pepper in the seasoned flour, then dip it into the beaten egg yolks, coating it evenly. Finally, gently fold the stuffed pepper into the beaten egg whites, coating it completely.

7. Carefully place the coated peppers in the hot oil and fry them until golden brown and crispy on all sides, about 3-4 minutes per side. Transfer the fried peppers to a paper towel-lined plate to drain excess oil.
8. In a saucepan, combine the chopped tomatoes, onion, garlic, jalapeño pepper (if using), and dried oregano. Cook the sauce over medium heat, stirring occasionally, until the tomatoes break down and the sauce thickens slightly. Season with salt and pepper to taste.
9. Serve the Chiles Rellenos hot, drizzled with the tomato sauce.

Enjoy your homemade Chiles Rellenos, a flavorful and satisfying dish that's sure to impress!

Beef Empanadas

Ingredients:

For the dough:

- 3 cups all-purpose flour
- 1 teaspoon salt
- 1/2 cup unsalted butter, cold and diced
- 1 large egg
- 1/2 cup cold water

For the filling:

- 500g (1 lb) ground beef
- 1 onion, finely chopped
- 2 cloves garlic, minced
- 1 bell pepper, diced
- 1 teaspoon ground cumin
- 1 teaspoon paprika
- 1/2 teaspoon dried oregano
- Salt and pepper to taste
- 1/2 cup frozen peas
- 1/2 cup pitted olives, sliced
- 1/4 cup raisins (optional)
- 2 tablespoons tomato paste
- 1/4 cup beef broth or water
- 2 hard-boiled eggs, chopped (optional)

Instructions:

1. To make the dough, sift the flour and salt into a large mixing bowl. Add the diced butter and use your fingers or a pastry cutter to rub the butter into the flour until the mixture resembles coarse crumbs.

2. In a separate bowl, beat the egg with the cold water. Gradually add the egg mixture to the flour mixture, stirring until a dough forms. If the dough is too dry, add more water, a tablespoon at a time.
3. Turn the dough out onto a floured surface and knead it gently until smooth. Wrap the dough in plastic wrap and refrigerate it for at least 30 minutes, or up to 1 hour.
4. While the dough is chilling, prepare the filling. In a large skillet, heat a tablespoon of oil over medium heat. Add the chopped onion and cook until softened, about 5 minutes. Add the minced garlic and diced bell pepper, and cook for another 2-3 minutes.
5. Add the ground beef to the skillet, breaking it up with a spoon. Cook the beef until browned, then drain any excess fat.
6. Stir in the ground cumin, paprika, dried oregano, salt, and pepper. Add the frozen peas, sliced olives, raisins (if using), tomato paste, and beef broth or water. Cook the mixture for another 5-7 minutes, or until the filling is thickened. Remove the skillet from the heat and let the filling cool slightly.
7. Preheat your oven to 200°C (400°F). Line a baking sheet with parchment paper.
8. On a floured surface, roll out the chilled dough to a thickness of about 1/4 inch. Use a round cutter or a glass to cut out circles of dough, about 4-5 inches in diameter.
9. Place a spoonful of the beef filling in the center of each dough circle. Add a few pieces of chopped hard-boiled egg (if using) on top of the filling.
10. Fold the dough over the filling to create a half-moon shape. Use a fork to press the edges of the dough together to seal the empanadas.
11. Place the filled empanadas on the prepared baking sheet. Brush the tops of the empanadas with beaten egg for a golden finish (optional).
12. Bake the empanadas in the preheated oven for 20-25 minutes, or until golden brown and crispy.
13. Remove the empanadas from the oven and let them cool slightly before serving.

Enjoy your homemade beef empanadas, a delicious and satisfying snack or meal!

Chicken Mole

Ingredients:

For the chicken:

- 1.5 kg (about 3 lbs) bone-in, skin-on chicken pieces (such as thighs and drumsticks)
- Salt and pepper to taste
- 2 tablespoons vegetable oil

For the mole sauce:

- 2 dried ancho chili peppers, stemmed and seeded
- 2 dried pasilla chili peppers, stemmed and seeded
- 2 dried guajillo chili peppers, stemmed and seeded
- 2 tablespoons vegetable oil
- 1 onion, chopped
- 3 cloves garlic, minced
- 1/2 cup almonds, toasted
- 1/4 cup raisins
- 1/4 cup sesame seeds, toasted
- 1/4 cup pumpkin seeds, toasted
- 1/4 cup peanuts, toasted
- 1/4 cup unsweetened cocoa powder
- 1 teaspoon ground cinnamon
- 1/2 teaspoon ground cloves
- 1/2 teaspoon ground coriander
- 1/2 teaspoon ground cumin
- 1/4 teaspoon ground nutmeg
- 1/4 teaspoon ground allspice
- 1/4 teaspoon ground black pepper
- 4 cups chicken broth
- 2 ounces (about 60g) unsweetened chocolate, chopped
- Salt to taste
- 2 tablespoons brown sugar or piloncillo (optional, for sweetness)

For serving:

- Cooked rice
- Warm tortillas or bread
- Sesame seeds and chopped cilantro for garnish (optional)

Instructions:

1. Season the chicken pieces with salt and pepper.
2. Heat 2 tablespoons of vegetable oil in a large Dutch oven or pot over medium-high heat. Add the chicken pieces in batches and cook until browned on all sides, about 5 minutes per side. Transfer the browned chicken to a plate and set aside.
3. In the same pot, add the dried chili peppers and toast them for a few minutes until fragrant. Remove the chili peppers from the pot and set them aside.
4. In the same pot, add 2 tablespoons of vegetable oil. Add the chopped onion and minced garlic, and cook until softened, about 5 minutes.
5. Add the toasted almonds, raisins, sesame seeds, pumpkin seeds, and peanuts to the pot. Cook, stirring frequently, for another 5 minutes.
6. Add the toasted chili peppers to the pot, along with the cocoa powder, ground cinnamon, ground cloves, ground coriander, ground cumin, ground nutmeg, ground allspice, and ground black pepper. Cook, stirring constantly, for 2-3 minutes to toast the spices.
7. Pour in the chicken broth and bring the mixture to a simmer. Let it simmer for 10-15 minutes, allowing the flavors to meld.
8. Use an immersion blender or transfer the mixture to a blender, and blend until smooth. If using a blender, be sure to vent the lid to allow steam to escape.
9. Once the sauce is smooth, return it to the pot. Stir in the chopped unsweetened chocolate and brown sugar or piloncillo (if using). Cook, stirring occasionally, until the chocolate is melted and the sauce has thickened slightly, about 5-10 minutes.
10. Taste the mole sauce and adjust the seasoning with salt and additional brown sugar or piloncillo if needed, to balance the flavors.
11. Return the browned chicken pieces to the pot, along with any accumulated juices. Spoon some of the mole sauce over the chicken to coat it evenly.
12. Cover the pot and let the chicken simmer in the mole sauce over low heat for 30-40 minutes, or until the chicken is cooked through and tender.

13. Serve the chicken mole hot, with cooked rice and warm tortillas or bread on the side. Garnish with sesame seeds and chopped cilantro if desired.

Enjoy your homemade chicken mole, a rich and flavorful dish that's sure to impress!

Fish Tacos

Ingredients:

For the fish:

- 1 lb (about 450g) firm white fish fillets (such as tilapia, cod, or mahi-mahi)
- 1 tablespoon olive oil
- 1 teaspoon chili powder
- 1/2 teaspoon cumin
- 1/2 teaspoon garlic powder
- Salt and pepper to taste
- Juice of 1 lime

For assembly:

- 8 small corn or flour tortillas
- Shredded cabbage or lettuce
- Pico de gallo or diced tomatoes
- Sliced avocado or guacamole
- Sour cream or chipotle mayo
- Fresh cilantro leaves (optional)
- Lime wedges for serving

Instructions:

1. Prepare the fish: Pat the fish fillets dry with paper towels. In a small bowl, mix together the olive oil, chili powder, cumin, garlic powder, salt, pepper, and lime juice. Rub this seasoning mixture all over the fish fillets, coating them evenly. Let the fish marinate for about 15-30 minutes.
2. Cook the fish: Heat a skillet or grill pan over medium-high heat. Add a little more olive oil to the pan if needed. Once hot, add the fish fillets and cook for 3-4 minutes per side, or until the fish is cooked through and flakes easily with a fork. Cooking time may vary depending on the thickness of the fillets.

3. Warm the tortillas: While the fish is cooking, warm the tortillas. You can do this by heating them in a dry skillet for about 30 seconds on each side or by wrapping them in foil and heating them in a low oven for a few minutes.
4. Assemble the tacos: Once the fish is cooked, break it into chunks using a fork. To assemble each taco, place some shredded cabbage or lettuce on a tortilla, top with pieces of fish, pico de gallo or diced tomatoes, sliced avocado or guacamole, and a dollop of sour cream or chipotle mayo. Sprinkle with fresh cilantro leaves if desired. Repeat with the remaining tortillas and ingredients.
5. Serve: Serve the fish tacos immediately, with lime wedges on the side for squeezing over the top. Enjoy!

Feel free to customize the toppings and seasonings to suit your taste preferences.

These fish tacos are versatile and can be easily adapted with your favorite ingredients!

Beef Tamales

Ingredients:

For the filling:

- 1 lb (about 450g) beef chuck roast, trimmed of excess fat and cut into small pieces
- 1 onion, diced
- 2 cloves garlic, minced
- 1 tablespoon vegetable oil
- 1 teaspoon ground cumin
- 1 teaspoon chili powder
- 1/2 teaspoon paprika
- Salt and pepper to taste
- 1 cup beef broth or water

For the masa dough:

- 2 cups masa harina (corn flour for tamales)
- 1 cup beef broth or water
- 1/2 cup vegetable shortening or lard
- 1 teaspoon baking powder
- Salt to taste

For assembling:

- Corn husks, soaked in warm water for at least 30 minutes to soften

Instructions:

1. Prepare the filling: In a large skillet, heat the vegetable oil over medium heat. Add the diced onion and minced garlic, and cook until softened, about 3-4 minutes. Add the beef pieces to the skillet and brown on all sides.

2. Season the beef: Sprinkle the cumin, chili powder, paprika, salt, and pepper over the beef in the skillet. Stir well to coat the beef evenly with the spices. Pour in the beef broth or water, reduce the heat to low, cover, and simmer for 1 to 1 1/2 hours, or until the beef is tender and can be easily shredded with a fork. Remove from heat and let it cool slightly.
3. Shred the beef: Once the beef is cool enough to handle, shred it using two forks or your fingers. Set aside.
4. Prepare the masa dough: In a large mixing bowl, combine the masa harina, beef broth or water, vegetable shortening or lard, baking powder, and salt. Mix until a soft dough forms. The consistency should be similar to that of peanut butter.
5. Assemble the tamales: Drain the corn husks from the water and pat them dry with paper towels. Take one corn husk and spread a thin layer of masa dough onto the center, leaving about 1 inch of space from the edges. Spoon some shredded beef filling down the center of the masa dough.
6. Fold the tamale: Fold one side of the corn husk over the filling, then fold the other side over to enclose it. Fold the narrow end of the corn husk up, then tie the tamale securely with a strip of corn husk or kitchen twine. Repeat with the remaining corn husks, masa dough, and beef filling.
7. Steam the tamales: Arrange the assembled tamales vertically in a steamer basket, open ends facing up. Place the steamer basket in a large pot filled with enough water to reach just below the bottom of the steamer. Cover the pot with a lid and steam the tamales for about 1 to 1 1/2 hours, or until the masa dough is firm and cooked through.
8. Serve: Once cooked, remove the tamales from the steamer and let them cool for a few minutes before serving. Unwrap the corn husks and enjoy the beef tamales warm with your favorite toppings such as salsa, sour cream, or guacamole.

These beef tamales are a labor of love, but the delicious flavors and comforting texture make them well worth the effort!

Chicken Tinga

Ingredients:

- 1 lb (about 450g) boneless, skinless chicken breasts or thighs
- 2 tablespoons vegetable oil
- 1 onion, finely chopped
- 3 cloves garlic, minced
- 2 chipotle peppers in adobo sauce, chopped (adjust to taste for spiciness)
- 1 (14 oz) can diced tomatoes
- 1 teaspoon dried oregano
- 1 teaspoon ground cumin
- 1/2 teaspoon smoked paprika
- Salt and pepper to taste
- 1/2 cup chicken broth or water
- Fresh cilantro, chopped (for garnish, optional)
- Lime wedges (for serving)

Instructions:

1. Cook the chicken: In a large skillet or pot, heat the vegetable oil over medium-high heat. Add the chicken breasts or thighs and cook until browned on both sides, about 5-7 minutes per side. Remove the chicken from the skillet and set aside.
2. Make the sauce: In the same skillet, add the chopped onion and minced garlic. Cook until softened and fragrant, about 3-4 minutes. Stir in the chopped chipotle peppers, diced tomatoes, dried oregano, ground cumin, smoked paprika, salt, and pepper. Cook for another 2-3 minutes, allowing the flavors to meld together.
3. Shred the chicken: Once the sauce is ready, return the cooked chicken to the skillet. Use two forks to shred the chicken directly in the sauce. Stir well to coat the chicken evenly with the sauce.
4. Simmer: Pour in the chicken broth or water, reduce the heat to low, cover the skillet, and simmer for 15-20 minutes, stirring occasionally, until the chicken is tender and the sauce has thickened slightly.
5. Serve: Once the chicken tinga is ready, garnish with chopped cilantro if desired and serve warm. You can use chicken tinga as a filling for tacos, tostadas, or

serve it over rice with beans. Squeeze fresh lime juice over the top before serving for an extra burst of flavor.

Enjoy your homemade chicken tinga with your favorite accompaniments and savor the smoky, spicy goodness of this classic Mexican dish!

Carne Asada

Ingredients:

- 2 lbs (about 900g) flank steak or skirt steak
- 1/4 cup orange juice
- 1/4 cup lime juice
- 1/4 cup soy sauce
- 1/4 cup olive oil
- 4 cloves garlic, minced
- 1 teaspoon ground cumin
- 1 teaspoon chili powder
- 1 teaspoon paprika
- 1/2 teaspoon dried oregano
- Salt and pepper to taste
- Fresh cilantro, chopped (for garnish, optional)
- Lime wedges (for serving)

Instructions:

1. Prepare the marinade: In a bowl, whisk together the orange juice, lime juice, soy sauce, olive oil, minced garlic, ground cumin, chili powder, paprika, dried oregano, salt, and pepper.
2. Marinate the steak: Place the flank steak or skirt steak in a shallow dish or a resealable plastic bag. Pour the marinade over the steak, making sure it's evenly coated. Cover the dish or seal the bag and refrigerate for at least 2 hours, or preferably overnight, to allow the flavors to penetrate the meat.
3. Preheat the grill: Preheat your grill to medium-high heat. If using a charcoal grill, wait until the coals are ashed over.
4. Grill the steak: Remove the steak from the marinade and discard any excess marinade. Place the steak on the preheated grill and cook for about 4-5 minutes per side for medium-rare, or longer if desired, depending on your preferred level of doneness and the thickness of the steak. Use a meat thermometer to ensure the internal temperature reaches your desired level of doneness (about 130-135°F or 55-57°C for medium-rare).

5. Rest and slice: Once cooked to your liking, transfer the steak to a cutting board and let it rest for a few minutes to allow the juices to redistribute. Slice the steak against the grain into thin strips.
6. Serve: Arrange the sliced carne asada on a platter, garnish with chopped cilantro if desired, and serve with lime wedges on the side. Carne asada is typically served with warm tortillas, rice, beans, salsa, guacamole, and other toppings for assembling tacos or burritos.

Enjoy your homemade carne asada with your favorite sides and toppings, and savor the delicious flavors of this classic grilled dish!

Beef Chimichangas

Ingredients:

For the beef filling:

- 1 lb (about 450g) lean ground beef
- 1 onion, finely chopped
- 2 cloves garlic, minced
- 1 bell pepper, diced
- 1 jalapeño pepper, seeded and diced (optional, for heat)
- 1 tablespoon vegetable oil
- 1 teaspoon ground cumin
- 1 teaspoon chili powder
- 1/2 teaspoon paprika
- Salt and pepper to taste
- 1/2 cup tomato sauce or diced tomatoes
- 1/4 cup beef broth or water
- 1/4 cup chopped fresh cilantro (optional)
- 1 cup shredded cheese (such as cheddar or Monterey Jack)

For assembling:

- 6 large flour tortillas
- Vegetable oil, for frying
- Sour cream, guacamole, salsa, shredded lettuce, diced tomatoes, for serving (optional)

Instructions:

1. Prepare the beef filling: In a large skillet, heat the vegetable oil over medium heat. Add the chopped onion and cook until softened, about 3-4 minutes. Add the minced garlic, diced bell pepper, and jalapeño pepper (if using), and cook for another 2-3 minutes until fragrant.

2. Add the ground beef to the skillet and cook, breaking it apart with a spoon, until browned and cooked through.
3. Season the beef: Sprinkle the ground cumin, chili powder, paprika, salt, and pepper over the beef in the skillet. Stir well to combine.
4. Add the tomato sauce or diced tomatoes and beef broth or water to the skillet. Stir to combine, then simmer for 5-10 minutes until the sauce has thickened slightly. Stir in the chopped cilantro, if using. Remove from heat and let the beef filling cool slightly.
5. Assemble the chimichangas: Place a few spoonfuls of the beef filling in the center of a flour tortilla. Sprinkle some shredded cheese over the top of the beef filling.
6. Fold the sides of the tortilla over the filling, then fold the bottom edge up and roll tightly to enclose the filling completely. Repeat with the remaining tortillas and beef filling.
7. Fry the chimichangas: In a large skillet or deep fryer, heat enough vegetable oil to submerge the chimichangas. Carefully place the chimichangas seam-side down in the hot oil and fry until golden brown and crispy, about 2-3 minutes per side. Use tongs to flip them halfway through frying.
8. Drain and serve: Once the chimichangas are golden and crispy, remove them from the oil and place them on a paper towel-lined plate to drain any excess oil.
9. Serve: Serve the beef chimichangas hot with your choice of toppings such as sour cream, guacamole, salsa, shredded lettuce, and diced tomatoes. Enjoy!

These homemade beef chimichangas are crispy on the outside, savory and flavorful on the inside, and perfect for a satisfying Tex-Mex meal at home!

Salsa Verde

Ingredients:

- 1 lb (about 450g) tomatillos, husked and rinsed
- 2-3 jalapeño peppers (adjust to taste for spiciness)
- 1 onion, chopped
- 2 cloves garlic
- 1/2 cup chopped fresh cilantro
- Juice of 1 lime
- Salt to taste

Instructions:

1. Roast the tomatillos and peppers: Preheat your broiler to high. Place the husked and rinsed tomatillos and jalapeño peppers on a baking sheet lined with aluminum foil. Broil for about 5-7 minutes, turning occasionally, until the tomatillos and peppers are charred and softened. Alternatively, you can roast them over an open flame on a gas stovetop or grill until charred.
2. Blend the ingredients: Once roasted, transfer the tomatillos, peppers, onion, garlic, cilantro, lime juice, and a pinch of salt to a blender or food processor. Blend until smooth. You can adjust the consistency of the salsa by adding a little water if it's too thick.
3. Season to taste: Taste the salsa and adjust the seasoning, adding more salt or lime juice if needed. You can also adjust the spiciness by adding more jalapeño peppers or removing the seeds and membranes for a milder flavor.
4. Serve: Transfer the salsa verde to a serving bowl or container. You can serve it immediately, or for best flavor, refrigerate it for at least 30 minutes to allow the flavors to meld together.
5. Enjoy: Salsa verde is delicious served with tortilla chips as a dip, or as a condiment for tacos, burritos, enchiladas, grilled meats, seafood, and more. It adds a bright and zesty flavor to any dish!

Feel free to customize this salsa verde recipe to suit your taste preferences by adjusting the level of spiciness or adding other ingredients like roasted garlic or extra cilantro. Enjoy your homemade salsa verde!

Guacamole

Ingredients:

- 2 ripe avocados
- 1/4 cup finely chopped onion
- 1/4 cup diced tomatoes (seeds and pulp removed)
- 2 tablespoons chopped fresh cilantro
- 1-2 tablespoons fresh lime juice (adjust to taste)
- 1 small jalapeño pepper, seeded and minced (optional, for heat)
- 1 clove garlic, minced
- Salt to taste

Instructions:

1. Prepare the avocados: Cut the avocados in half lengthwise and remove the pits. Scoop the flesh into a mixing bowl.
2. Mash the avocados: Use a fork to mash the avocado flesh until smooth or slightly chunky, depending on your preference. If you prefer a smoother texture, you can use a potato masher or the back of a spoon.
3. Add the remaining ingredients: Add the finely chopped onion, diced tomatoes, chopped cilantro, lime juice, minced jalapeño pepper (if using), minced garlic, and a pinch of salt to the mashed avocado.
4. Mix well: Gently stir all the ingredients together until evenly combined. Be careful not to overmix, as you want to maintain some texture in the guacamole.
5. Taste and adjust seasoning: Taste the guacamole and adjust the seasoning as needed, adding more lime juice or salt if desired.
6. Serve: Transfer the guacamole to a serving bowl. You can garnish it with additional chopped cilantro or a sprinkle of paprika for presentation if desired.
7. Enjoy: Serve the guacamole immediately with tortilla chips, fresh vegetables, or as a topping for tacos, burritos, quesadillas, or any of your favorite Mexican dishes. Guacamole is best enjoyed fresh, but you can store leftovers in an airtight container in the refrigerator for up to one day, though it's best consumed soon after making for optimal flavor and texture.

Feel free to customize this guacamole recipe to suit your taste preferences by adjusting the amount of lime juice, cilantro, or jalapeño pepper, or by adding other ingredients like diced red onion or minced serrano peppers for extra heat. Enjoy your homemade guacamole!

Pico de Gallo

Ingredients:

- 4 medium ripe tomatoes, diced
- 1/2 cup finely chopped onion (white, red, or yellow)
- 1/4 cup chopped fresh cilantro
- 1 jalapeño pepper, seeded and finely chopped (adjust to taste)
- Juice of 1 lime
- Salt to taste

Instructions:

1. Prepare the ingredients: Wash and dice the tomatoes, finely chop the onion, chop the cilantro, and finely chop the jalapeño pepper, removing the seeds and membranes if you prefer a milder salsa.
2. Combine the ingredients: In a mixing bowl, combine the diced tomatoes, chopped onion, chopped cilantro, and finely chopped jalapeño pepper.
3. Add lime juice and salt: Squeeze the juice of one lime over the tomato mixture. Season with salt to taste. Start with a small amount of salt and adjust according to your preference.
4. Mix well: Gently toss all the ingredients together until evenly combined. Be careful not to overmix, as you want to maintain the texture of the diced tomatoes.
5. Taste and adjust seasoning: Taste the pico de gallo and adjust the seasoning as needed, adding more lime juice or salt if desired.
6. Serve: Transfer the pico de gallo to a serving bowl. You can garnish it with additional chopped cilantro if desired.
7. Enjoy: Serve the pico de gallo immediately as a dip with tortilla chips, or use it as a topping for tacos, burritos, quesadillas, grilled meats, seafood, or any of your favorite Mexican dishes. Pico de gallo is best enjoyed fresh, but you can store leftovers in an airtight container in the refrigerator for up to two days.

Feel free to customize this pico de gallo recipe to suit your taste preferences by adjusting the amount of onion, cilantro, jalapeño pepper, or lime juice, or by adding other ingredients like diced bell peppers, avocado, or mango for a unique twist. Enjoy your homemade pico de gallo!

Mexican Rice

Ingredients:

- 1 cup long-grain white rice
- 1 tablespoon vegetable oil or olive oil
- 1 onion, finely chopped
- 2 cloves garlic, minced
- 1 teaspoon ground cumin
- 1 teaspoon chili powder
- 1/2 teaspoon paprika
- 1/2 teaspoon dried oregano
- 1 (14 oz) can diced tomatoes, undrained
- 1 3/4 cups chicken broth or vegetable broth
- Salt and pepper to taste
- Chopped fresh cilantro (optional, for garnish)
- Lime wedges (optional, for serving)

Instructions:

1. Rinse the rice: Place the rice in a fine mesh strainer and rinse under cold water until the water runs clear. This helps remove excess starch and prevents the rice from becoming sticky.
2. Sauté the aromatics: In a large skillet or saucepan, heat the vegetable oil over medium heat. Add the finely chopped onion and cook until softened, about 3-4 minutes. Add the minced garlic and cook for another 1-2 minutes until fragrant.
3. Toast the rice: Add the rinsed rice to the skillet with the onion and garlic. Cook, stirring frequently, for about 3-4 minutes until the rice is lightly toasted and golden brown.
4. Add the spices and tomatoes: Sprinkle the ground cumin, chili powder, paprika, and dried oregano over the rice. Stir well to coat the rice evenly with the spices. Add the diced tomatoes, including the liquid from the can, and stir to combine.
5. Simmer the rice: Pour the chicken broth or vegetable broth into the skillet, stirring to combine. Season with salt and pepper to taste. Bring the mixture to a simmer, then reduce the heat to low. Cover the skillet with a lid and let the rice cook for about 18-20 minutes, or until the liquid is absorbed and the rice is tender.

6. Fluff and garnish: Once the rice is cooked, remove the skillet from the heat and let it sit, covered, for a few minutes. Fluff the rice with a fork to separate the grains. If desired, garnish with chopped fresh cilantro before serving.
7. Serve: Transfer the Mexican rice to a serving dish and serve warm. You can accompany it with lime wedges on the side for squeezing over the rice for an extra burst of flavor.

Enjoy your homemade Mexican rice as a delicious side dish with your favorite Mexican-inspired meals!

Refried Beans

Ingredients:

- 2 cups cooked pinto beans (or black beans), drained and rinsed
- 2 tablespoons vegetable oil or lard
- 1/2 onion, finely chopped
- 2 cloves garlic, minced
- 1 teaspoon ground cumin
- 1/2 teaspoon chili powder
- Salt to taste
- Water (as needed)
- Optional toppings: shredded cheese, chopped cilantro, diced tomatoes, sliced jalapeños, sour cream, or crumbled cotija cheese

Instructions:

1. Heat the oil: In a large skillet or saucepan, heat the vegetable oil or lard over medium heat.
2. Sauté the aromatics: Add the finely chopped onion to the skillet and cook until softened, about 3-4 minutes. Add the minced garlic and cook for another 1-2 minutes until fragrant.
3. Mash the beans: Add the cooked pinto beans to the skillet. Use a potato masher or the back of a spoon to mash the beans until they are mostly smooth, leaving some texture if desired.
4. Season the beans: Sprinkle the ground cumin, chili powder, and salt over the mashed beans. Stir well to combine, allowing the seasonings to meld with the beans.
5. Fry the beans: Cook the mashed beans, stirring frequently, for about 5-7 minutes until they are heated through and slightly thickened. If the beans seem too dry, you can add a splash of water to achieve your desired consistency.
6. Taste and adjust seasoning: Taste the refried beans and adjust the seasoning as needed, adding more salt or spices if desired.
7. Serve: Transfer the refried beans to a serving dish. You can serve them as a side dish or as a filling for tacos, burritos, tostadas, or enchiladas. Top with your favorite toppings such as shredded cheese, chopped cilantro, diced tomatoes, sliced jalapeños, sour cream, or crumbled cotija cheese.

8. Enjoy: Serve the refried beans warm and enjoy their creamy texture and savory flavor alongside your favorite Mexican dishes!

Homemade refried beans are delicious, versatile, and easy to make, allowing you to customize them to suit your taste preferences.

Chile Con Carne

Ingredients:

- 1 lb (about 450g) ground beef or cubed beef chuck
- 2 tablespoons vegetable oil
- 1 onion, chopped
- 2 cloves garlic, minced
- 1 bell pepper, diced
- 2 jalapeño peppers, seeded and diced (adjust to taste for spiciness)
- 1 (14 oz) can diced tomatoes
- 1 (14 oz) can kidney beans, drained and rinsed
- 2 cups beef broth
- 2 tablespoons chili powder
- 1 teaspoon ground cumin
- 1 teaspoon paprika
- 1/2 teaspoon dried oregano
- Salt and pepper to taste
- Optional toppings: shredded cheese, chopped cilantro, diced onions, sour cream, avocado slices, lime wedges

Instructions:

1. Brown the beef: In a large pot or Dutch oven, heat the vegetable oil over medium-high heat. Add the ground beef or cubed beef chuck and cook, breaking it apart with a spoon, until browned.
2. Sauté the aromatics: Add the chopped onion, minced garlic, diced bell pepper, and diced jalapeño peppers to the pot with the browned beef. Cook, stirring occasionally, until the vegetables are softened, about 5-7 minutes.
3. Add the tomatoes and beans: Pour in the diced tomatoes (including the liquid from the can) and kidney beans. Stir to combine.
4. Season the chili: Add the beef broth, chili powder, ground cumin, paprika, dried oregano, salt, and pepper to the pot. Stir well to combine all the ingredients.
5. Simmer the chili: Bring the chile con carne to a simmer, then reduce the heat to low. Cover the pot with a lid and let the chili simmer for about 30-45 minutes, stirring occasionally, until the flavors have melded together and the chili has thickened to your desired consistency.

6. Taste and adjust seasoning: Taste the chili and adjust the seasoning as needed, adding more salt, chili powder, or other spices to suit your taste preferences.
7. Serve: Ladle the chili con carne into bowls and serve hot. You can garnish each bowl with shredded cheese, chopped cilantro, diced onions, sour cream, avocado slices, or a squeeze of lime juice, if desired.
8. Enjoy: Serve the chili con carne with warm tortillas, cornbread, or rice for a complete and satisfying meal. Enjoy the hearty and comforting flavors of this classic dish!

Feel free to customize this chile con carne recipe by adjusting the level of spiciness, adding more vegetables, or incorporating different types of beans.

Chipotle Chicken

Ingredients:

- 4 boneless, skinless chicken breasts
- 2 chipotle peppers in adobo sauce
- 2 cloves garlic
- 2 tablespoons lime juice
- 2 tablespoons olive oil
- 1 teaspoon ground cumin
- 1 teaspoon dried oregano
- 1/2 teaspoon smoked paprika
- Salt and pepper to taste
- Chopped fresh cilantro (for garnish, optional)
- Lime wedges (for serving)

Instructions:

1. Prepare the chipotle marinade: In a blender or food processor, combine the chipotle peppers in adobo sauce, garlic cloves, lime juice, olive oil, ground cumin, dried oregano, smoked paprika, salt, and pepper. Blend until smooth.
2. Marinate the chicken: Place the chicken breasts in a shallow dish or a resealable plastic bag. Pour the chipotle marinade over the chicken, making sure it's evenly coated. Cover the dish or seal the bag and refrigerate for at least 30 minutes, or preferably overnight, to allow the flavors to penetrate the chicken.
3. Cook the chicken: Preheat your grill or grill pan to medium-high heat. Remove the chicken from the marinade and discard any excess marinade. Grill the chicken breasts for about 6-8 minutes per side, or until they are cooked through and no longer pink in the center. Cooking time may vary depending on the thickness of the chicken breasts.
4. Rest and garnish: Once cooked, transfer the chicken breasts to a cutting board and let them rest for a few minutes. Garnish with chopped fresh cilantro, if desired.
5. Serve: Slice the chipotle chicken breasts and serve them hot with lime wedges on the side for squeezing over the top. You can enjoy chipotle chicken as a main dish alongside rice, beans, or grilled vegetables, or use it as a filling for tacos, burritos, salads, or wraps.

6. Enjoy: Serve the chipotle chicken immediately and savor the smoky, spicy flavors of this delicious dish!

Feel free to adjust the level of spiciness by adding more or fewer chipotle peppers to the marinade, and customize the seasoning to suit your taste preferences. Chipotle chicken is a versatile and satisfying dish that's perfect for a quick and flavorful meal any day of the week!

Shrimp Ceviche

Ingredients:

- 1 lb (about 450g) raw shrimp, peeled and deveined
- 4-5 limes, juiced (enough to cover the shrimp)
- 1/2 red onion, finely chopped
- 1-2 tomatoes, diced
- 1 cucumber, peeled and diced
- 1 jalapeño pepper, seeded and finely chopped (adjust to taste)
- 1/4 cup chopped fresh cilantro
- 1 avocado, diced
- Salt and pepper to taste
- Tortilla chips or tostadas, for serving

Instructions:

1. Prepare the shrimp: Bring a pot of salted water to a boil. Add the raw shrimp and cook for about 2-3 minutes until they turn pink and opaque. Drain the shrimp and transfer them to a bowl of ice water to stop the cooking process. Once cooled, drain the shrimp and pat them dry with paper towels.
2. Marinate the shrimp: Cut the cooked shrimp into bite-sized pieces and place them in a shallow dish. Pour the freshly squeezed lime juice over the shrimp, making sure they are completely submerged. Cover the dish with plastic wrap and refrigerate for about 30 minutes to 1 hour to allow the shrimp to "cook" in the citrus juice. The shrimp will turn opaque and firm when ready.
3. Prepare the vegetables: While the shrimp is marinating, prepare the vegetables. Finely chop the red onion, dice the tomatoes, peel and dice the cucumber, finely chop the jalapeño pepper (remove seeds and membranes for less heat if desired), and chop the fresh cilantro. Place the prepared vegetables in a large mixing bowl.
4. Combine the ceviche: Once the shrimp is "cooked" in the lime juice, drain off most of the excess liquid, leaving just enough to keep the ceviche moist. Add the marinated shrimp to the bowl with the prepared vegetables. Gently toss everything together until evenly combined.
5. Season the ceviche: Season the shrimp ceviche with salt and pepper to taste. You can also add additional lime juice if desired for extra acidity.

6. Add avocado: Just before serving, gently fold in the diced avocado to avoid it from browning.
7. Serve: Transfer the shrimp ceviche to a serving bowl or individual dishes. Serve immediately with tortilla chips or tostadas for scooping up the ceviche.
8. Enjoy: Enjoy your homemade shrimp ceviche as a refreshing appetizer or light meal, perfect for warm weather days!

Feel free to customize this shrimp ceviche recipe by adding other ingredients such as diced mango, pineapple, or serrano peppers for extra flavor and heat. Adjust the seasoning and spiciness to suit your taste preferences.

Chilaquiles

Ingredients:

- 8 corn tortillas, cut into triangles or strips
- Vegetable oil, for frying
- 2 cups salsa (red or green)
- 1/2 onion, finely chopped
- 2 cloves garlic, minced
- 1 jalapeño pepper, seeded and minced (optional, for heat)
- 1 cup cooked shredded chicken (optional)
- 1/2 cup shredded cheese (such as Monterey Jack or Mexican blend)
- Salt and pepper to taste
- Garnishes: chopped cilantro, sliced avocado, crema or sour cream, crumbled cotija cheese, lime wedges, fried or scrambled eggs

Instructions:

1. Fry the tortillas: In a large skillet, heat about 1/4 inch of vegetable oil over medium-high heat. Once the oil is hot, add the tortilla triangles or strips in batches, frying until golden and crispy, about 1-2 minutes per side. Use a slotted spoon to transfer the fried tortillas to a paper towel-lined plate to drain any excess oil.
2. Make the sauce: In the same skillet, heat a little more oil if needed over medium heat. Add the finely chopped onion and cook until softened, about 3-4 minutes. Add the minced garlic and jalapeño pepper (if using), and cook for another 1-2 minutes until fragrant. Pour in the salsa and stir to combine. Bring the sauce to a simmer and let it cook for about 5 minutes to allow the flavors to meld together. Season with salt and pepper to taste.
3. Simmer the chilaquiles: Once the sauce is ready, add the fried tortilla strips to the skillet, tossing them gently to coat evenly with the sauce. If using shredded chicken, add it to the skillet and stir to combine. Let the chilaquiles simmer in the sauce for about 3-5 minutes, until the tortillas soften slightly but still retain some texture.
4. Add cheese: Sprinkle the shredded cheese over the top of the chilaquiles. Cover the skillet with a lid and let it cook for another 2-3 minutes, or until the cheese is melted and bubbly.

5. Serve: Once the cheese is melted, remove the skillet from the heat. Transfer the chilaquiles to serving plates or a serving platter. Garnish with chopped cilantro, sliced avocado, crema or sour cream, crumbled cotija cheese, and lime wedges. Serve immediately, with fried or scrambled eggs on top if desired.
6. Enjoy: Enjoy your homemade chilaquiles as a hearty and satisfying breakfast, brunch, or any time of the day!

Chilaquiles can be customized with your favorite toppings and variations. You can use red or green salsa depending on your preference, and adjust the level of spiciness by adding more or fewer jalapeños. Feel free to make it vegetarian by omitting the chicken and adding extra vegetables.

Chicken Pozole

Ingredients:

- 1 lb (about 450g) boneless, skinless chicken breasts or thighs
- 1 onion, chopped
- 4 cloves garlic, minced
- 1 tablespoon vegetable oil
- 6 cups chicken broth
- 2 (15 oz) cans hominy, drained and rinsed
- 1 (14.5 oz) can diced tomatoes
- 2 dried ancho chilies, stemmed and seeded
- 1 teaspoon dried oregano
- 1 teaspoon ground cumin
- Salt and pepper to taste
- Optional toppings: shredded cabbage or lettuce, sliced radishes, chopped cilantro, diced avocado, lime wedges, thinly sliced jalapeños, tortilla chips or tostadas

Instructions:

1. Cook the chicken: In a large pot or Dutch oven, heat the vegetable oil over medium-high heat. Add the chopped onion and minced garlic, and cook until softened and fragrant, about 3-4 minutes. Add the chicken breasts or thighs to the pot and cook until browned on both sides, about 5-7 minutes.
2. Make the broth: Pour in the chicken broth and add the drained hominy to the pot. Stir in the diced tomatoes, dried oregano, ground cumin, dried ancho chilies, salt, and pepper. Bring the mixture to a boil, then reduce the heat to low. Cover the pot and let the soup simmer for about 20-25 minutes, until the chicken is cooked through and tender.
3. Shred the chicken: Once the chicken is cooked, remove it from the pot and transfer it to a cutting board. Use two forks to shred the chicken into bite-sized pieces. Return the shredded chicken to the pot.
4. Adjust seasoning: Taste the pozole and adjust the seasoning as needed, adding more salt and pepper if desired. You can also remove the dried ancho chilies if you prefer less heat, or leave them in for extra flavor.

5. Serve: Ladle the chicken pozole into serving bowls. Serve hot, garnished with your choice of toppings such as shredded cabbage or lettuce, sliced radishes, chopped cilantro, diced avocado, lime wedges, thinly sliced jalapeños, and tortilla chips or tostadas on the side.
6. Enjoy: Enjoy your homemade chicken pozole as a comforting and satisfying meal, perfect for cold days or any time you're craving a flavorful soup!

Feel free to customize this chicken pozole recipe to suit your taste preferences by adjusting the level of spiciness, adding more vegetables, or incorporating other ingredients such as diced onions, carrots, or bell peppers.

Birria

Ingredients:

For the Birria:

- 3 lbs (about 1.4 kg) beef chuck roast or beef brisket, cut into large chunks
- 2 dried guajillo chilies
- 2 dried ancho chilies
- 2 dried pasilla chilies
- 4 cups beef broth
- 1 onion, chopped
- 4 cloves garlic, minced
- 1 tablespoon ground cumin
- 1 tablespoon dried oregano
- 1 teaspoon ground cloves
- 1 teaspoon ground cinnamon
- Salt and pepper to taste
- 2 bay leaves

For Serving:

- Corn tortillas
- Chopped onion
- Chopped cilantro
- Lime wedges
- Sliced radishes
- Salsa or hot sauce (optional)

Instructions:

1. Prepare the dried chilies: Remove the stems and seeds from the dried guajillo, ancho, and pasilla chilies. Heat a dry skillet over medium heat and toast the chilies for a few seconds on each side until they become fragrant. Be careful not

to burn them. Transfer the toasted chilies to a bowl and cover them with hot water. Let them soak for about 20-30 minutes until softened.
2. Make the birria sauce: Once the dried chilies are softened, transfer them to a blender or food processor along with a cup of the soaking liquid. Blend until smooth, adding more soaking liquid as needed to achieve a smooth consistency.
3. Brown the beef: Season the beef chunks with salt and pepper. Heat a large pot or Dutch oven over medium-high heat and add a little oil. Brown the beef chunks on all sides, working in batches if necessary. Remove the browned beef from the pot and set it aside.
4. Cook the aromatics: In the same pot, add chopped onion and minced garlic. Cook until softened and fragrant, about 3-4 minutes.
5. Simmer the birria: Return the browned beef to the pot. Add the blended chili mixture, beef broth, ground cumin, dried oregano, ground cloves, ground cinnamon, and bay leaves. Stir to combine.
6. Braise the beef: Bring the mixture to a simmer, then reduce the heat to low. Cover the pot and let the birria simmer gently for 2-3 hours, or until the beef is tender and falls apart easily.
7. Serve: Once the beef is tender, remove it from the pot and shred it into bite-sized pieces using two forks. Return the shredded beef to the pot and stir to combine with the sauce.
8. Serve the birria: Serve the beef birria hot, either as a stew or in tacos. To serve in tacos, heat corn tortillas on a griddle or skillet until warm and pliable. Fill each tortilla with a generous portion of beef birria and top with chopped onion, chopped cilantro, a squeeze of lime juice, and sliced radishes. Serve with salsa or hot sauce on the side, if desired.
9. Enjoy: Enjoy your homemade beef birria, savoring its rich and complex flavors!

Feel free to adjust the spiciness of the birria by adding more or fewer dried chilies, or by incorporating additional spices to suit your taste preferences.

Huevos Rancheros

Ingredients:

- 4 corn or flour tortillas
- 4 eggs
- 1 cup refried beans (homemade or store-bought)
- 1 cup ranchero sauce (see recipe below)
- 1/2 cup shredded cheese (such as Monterey Jack or Cheddar)
- Chopped fresh cilantro, for garnish (optional)
- Sliced avocado, for garnish (optional)
- Lime wedges, for serving (optional)

For the Ranchero Sauce:

- 2 tablespoons vegetable oil
- 1 onion, finely chopped
- 2 cloves garlic, minced
- 1 jalapeño pepper, seeded and minced
- 1 (14.5 oz) can diced tomatoes
- 1 teaspoon ground cumin
- 1 teaspoon chili powder
- Salt and pepper to taste

Instructions:

1. Prepare the ranchero sauce: In a large skillet, heat the vegetable oil over medium heat. Add the finely chopped onion and cook until softened, about 3-4 minutes. Add the minced garlic and jalapeño pepper, and cook for another 1-2 minutes until fragrant.
2. Add the diced tomatoes (including the liquid from the can), ground cumin, chili powder, salt, and pepper to the skillet. Stir to combine, and let the sauce simmer for about 10-15 minutes, stirring occasionally, until it thickens slightly.
3. While the sauce is simmering, warm the tortillas: Heat a griddle or skillet over medium heat. Warm the tortillas on the griddle or skillet for about 1 minute on

each side until they are heated through and pliable. Keep the tortillas warm by wrapping them in a clean kitchen towel or aluminum foil.
4. Fry the eggs: In a separate skillet, heat a little oil over medium heat. Crack the eggs into the skillet and cook them to your desired doneness. For traditional Huevos Rancheros, cook the eggs sunny-side up or over-easy, keeping the yolks runny.
5. Assemble the Huevos Rancheros: Place a warm tortilla on each serving plate. Spread a layer of refried beans over the tortillas. Top each tortilla with a fried egg. Spoon ranchero sauce over the eggs, covering them generously. Sprinkle shredded cheese over the top.
6. Garnish and serve: Garnish the Huevos Rancheros with chopped fresh cilantro and sliced avocado, if desired. Serve immediately, with lime wedges on the side for squeezing over the top.
7. Enjoy: Serve the Huevos Rancheros hot and enjoy the delicious combination of flavors and textures!

Huevos Rancheros can be customized to suit your taste preferences. You can add additional toppings such as sliced jalapeños, diced onions, or crumbled cotija cheese. Serve it with a side of Mexican rice, refried beans, or fresh salsa for a complete and satisfying meal.

Tostadas

Ingredients:

- Corn tortillas (6-inch size)
- Vegetable oil, for frying (if making fried tostadas)
- Refried beans (homemade or store-bought)
- Cooked shredded chicken, beef, pork, or seafood (optional)
- Chopped lettuce or shredded cabbage
- Diced tomatoes
- Sliced avocado or guacamole
- Crumbled queso fresco or shredded cheese (such as Monterey Jack or Cheddar)
- Salsa or hot sauce
- Sour cream or Mexican crema
- Chopped fresh cilantro
- Lime wedges, for serving (optional)

Instructions:

1. Prepare the tortillas: If making fried tostadas, heat about 1/2 inch of vegetable oil in a large skillet or frying pan over medium-high heat. Once the oil is hot, fry the tortillas one at a time, turning them occasionally with tongs, until they are golden and crispy, about 1-2 minutes per side. Drain the fried tortillas on paper towels to remove excess oil.
If making baked tostadas, preheat your oven to 400°F (200°C). Arrange the corn tortillas in a single layer on a baking sheet. Lightly brush both sides of the tortillas with vegetable oil. Bake in the preheated oven for about 8-10 minutes, flipping halfway through, until the tortillas are crisp and lightly golden.
2. Assemble the tostadas: Once the tortillas are crispy, spread a layer of refried beans on each tortilla. Top the beans with cooked shredded chicken, beef, pork, or seafood, if using. Add chopped lettuce or shredded cabbage, diced tomatoes, sliced avocado or guacamole, and crumbled queso fresco or shredded cheese.
3. Garnish and serve: Drizzle salsa or hot sauce over the tostadas, and add dollops of sour cream or Mexican crema. Sprinkle chopped fresh cilantro over the top for extra flavor and color. Serve the tostadas immediately, with lime wedges on the side for squeezing over the top, if desired.

4. Enjoy: Enjoy your homemade tostadas as a delicious and satisfying meal or snack!

Tostadas are versatile and customizable, so feel free to add or omit ingredients according to your taste preferences. You can also experiment with different toppings such as sliced radishes, pickled onions, jalapeño slices, or grilled vegetables. Serve the tostadas alongside rice and beans for a complete and hearty meal.

Sopa de Lima

Ingredients:

- 2 tablespoons vegetable oil
- 1 onion, chopped
- 2 cloves garlic, minced
- 2 tomatoes, chopped
- 1 bell pepper, chopped
- 1 jalapeño pepper, seeded and minced (optional, for heat)
- 6 cups chicken or vegetable broth
- 2 cups shredded cooked chicken
- 1 teaspoon ground cumin
- 1 teaspoon dried oregano
- 1/2 teaspoon ground coriander
- 1/4 cup freshly squeezed lime juice
- Salt and pepper to taste
- Corn tortillas, sliced into strips
- Avocado slices, for garnish
- Fresh cilantro leaves, for garnish
- Lime wedges, for serving

Instructions:

1. In a large pot or Dutch oven, heat the vegetable oil over medium heat. Add the chopped onion and cook until softened, about 3-4 minutes. Add the minced garlic and cook for another minute until fragrant.
2. Stir in the chopped tomatoes, bell pepper, and jalapeño pepper (if using). Cook for another 5 minutes, until the vegetables are softened.
3. Pour in the chicken or vegetable broth and bring the mixture to a simmer.
4. Add the shredded cooked chicken to the pot, along with the ground cumin, dried oregano, and ground coriander. Stir well to combine.
5. Let the soup simmer for about 15-20 minutes, allowing the flavors to meld together.
6. Stir in the freshly squeezed lime juice, and season the soup with salt and pepper to taste.

7. While the soup is simmering, prepare the tortilla strips. Heat a little oil in a skillet over medium-high heat. Fry the tortilla strips until golden and crispy. Drain them on paper towels and season with salt.
8. Serve the Sopa de Lima hot, garnished with avocado slices, fresh cilantro leaves, and crispy tortilla strips. Serve with lime wedges on the side for squeezing over the soup.
9. Enjoy your homemade Sopa de Lima, savoring its bright and zesty flavors!

Feel free to customize this Sopa de Lima recipe according to your preferences. You can adjust the level of spiciness by adding more or less jalapeño pepper, and you can also add extra garnishes such as diced red onion or crumbled cotija cheese.

Tamales de Elote

Ingredients:

For the Corn Masa:

- 4 cups fresh corn kernels (from about 6-8 ears of corn)
- 1/2 cup cornmeal or masa harina
- 1/4 cup granulated sugar
- 1/4 cup unsalted butter, melted
- 1 teaspoon baking powder
- 1/2 teaspoon salt

For the Filling:

- 1 cup fresh corn kernels (from about 2 ears of corn)
- 1/4 cup granulated sugar
- 1/4 cup unsalted butter, melted
- 1/4 cup milk or cream
- 1/4 teaspoon ground cinnamon (optional)

For Assembly:

- Dried corn husks, soaked in warm water for about 30 minutes to soften
- Kitchen twine or strips of soaked corn husks for tying

Instructions:

1. Prepare the Corn Masa:
    - In a blender or food processor, combine the fresh corn kernels, cornmeal or masa harina, granulated sugar, melted butter, baking powder, and salt. Blend until smooth, adding a little water if needed to achieve a thick but spreadable consistency.
2. Prepare the Filling:

- In a separate bowl, combine the fresh corn kernels, granulated sugar, melted butter, milk or cream, and ground cinnamon (if using). Mix well to combine.

3. Assemble the Tamales:
   - Spread a thin layer of the corn masa mixture onto the center of a softened corn husk, leaving a border around the edges. Spoon a small amount of the corn filling onto the center of the masa.
4. Fold the sides of the corn husk over the filling to enclose it, then fold up the bottom of the husk. Tie the tamale with kitchen twine or strips of soaked corn husks to secure it.
5. Steam the Tamales:
   - Arrange the assembled tamales upright in a steamer basket, with the open ends facing up. Make sure they are tightly packed to prevent them from unfolding during steaming.
   - Fill the bottom of the steamer pot with water, making sure it doesn't touch the tamales. Bring the water to a simmer over medium heat, then cover the steamer basket with a lid.
   - Steam the tamales for about 45-60 minutes, or until the masa is firm and cooked through. Check the water level periodically and add more water as needed to maintain the steam.
6. Serve:
   - Once the tamales are cooked, remove them from the steamer and let them cool slightly before serving. Unwrap the tamales from the corn husks and serve warm.
7. Enjoy your homemade Tamales de Elote as a delicious sweet treat or snack!

These Tamales de Elote are perfect for enjoying on their own, or you can serve them with a dollop of whipped cream or a sprinkle of powdered sugar for extra sweetness. They're a delightful way to savor the flavors of fresh corn in a traditional Mexican dish.

Beef Barbacoa

Ingredients:

- 3 lbs (about 1.4 kg) beef chuck roast or brisket, trimmed of excess fat and cut into large chunks
- 1 onion, chopped
- 4 cloves garlic, minced
- 1/4 cup fresh lime juice
- 1/4 cup apple cider vinegar
- 2 chipotle peppers in adobo sauce, minced
- 1 tablespoon ground cumin
- 1 tablespoon dried oregano
- 2 teaspoons smoked paprika
- 1 teaspoon ground cloves
- 1 teaspoon ground cinnamon
- 1/2 teaspoon ground black pepper
- 1 cup beef broth or water
- Salt to taste
- Fresh cilantro, chopped (for garnish, optional)
- Lime wedges (for serving, optional)

Instructions:

1. Prepare the marinade: In a blender or food processor, combine the chopped onion, minced garlic, fresh lime juice, apple cider vinegar, minced chipotle peppers, ground cumin, dried oregano, smoked paprika, ground cloves, ground cinnamon, ground black pepper, and beef broth or water. Blend until smooth.
2. Marinate the beef: Place the beef chunks in a large bowl or resealable plastic bag. Pour the marinade over the beef, making sure it's evenly coated. Cover the bowl or seal the bag, and refrigerate for at least 4 hours, or preferably overnight, to allow the flavors to penetrate the meat.
3. Slow-cook the beef: Preheat your oven to 325°F (160°C). Transfer the marinated beef and marinade to a Dutch oven or large oven-safe pot with a lid. Season the beef with salt to taste. Cover the pot with a lid and place it in the preheated oven.
4. Cook the beef for about 3-4 hours, or until the meat is tender and easily falls apart when shredded with a fork. Check the beef occasionally and add more liquid (such as beef broth or water) if needed to prevent it from drying out.

5. Shred the beef: Once the beef is cooked and tender, remove it from the oven. Use two forks to shred the beef into bite-sized pieces. Stir the shredded beef to coat it with the flavorful cooking liquid.
6. Serve: Serve the beef barbacoa hot, garnished with chopped fresh cilantro, if desired. Serve with lime wedges on the side for squeezing over the beef for an extra burst of flavor.
7. Enjoy your homemade beef barbacoa as a delicious filling for tacos, burritos, quesadillas, or served over rice or salad!

Beef barbacoa is a versatile and flavorful dish that's perfect for feeding a crowd or enjoying as leftovers throughout the week. The slow-cooking process allows the beef to become incredibly tender and infused with the rich and aromatic spices, resulting in a truly satisfying meal.

Mexican Street Corn (Elote)

Ingredients:

- 4 ears of corn, husked
- 1/4 cup mayonnaise
- 1/4 cup sour cream or Mexican crema
- 1/4 cup finely chopped cilantro
- 1 clove garlic, minced
- 1/4 teaspoon chili powder (adjust to taste)
- 1/4 teaspoon ground cumin
- 1/4 teaspoon smoked paprika
- 1/2 cup crumbled cotija cheese or grated Parmesan cheese
- Lime wedges, for serving
- Additional chopped cilantro, for garnish (optional)

Instructions:

1. Grill the corn: Preheat your grill to medium-high heat. Place the husked corn directly on the grill grates. Grill the corn, turning occasionally, until it is cooked and slightly charred on all sides, about 10-12 minutes.
2. Prepare the creamy mixture: In a small bowl, combine the mayonnaise, sour cream or Mexican crema, finely chopped cilantro, minced garlic, chili powder, ground cumin, and smoked paprika. Stir until well combined.
3. Coat the corn: Once the corn is grilled, remove it from the grill and place it on a serving platter. Use a basting brush or spoon to generously coat each ear of corn with the creamy mixture, making sure to cover all sides.
4. Add toppings: Sprinkle crumbled cotija cheese or grated Parmesan cheese over the creamy mixture on each ear of corn. You can adjust the amount of cheese to your preference.
5. Serve: Serve the Mexican street corn hot, garnished with lime wedges on the side for squeezing over the top. Optionally, sprinkle additional chopped cilantro over the corn for extra freshness and flavor.
6. Enjoy: Enjoy your homemade Mexican street corn as a delicious and flavorful side dish or snack!

Mexican street corn is a classic and irresistible treat that's perfect for summer cookouts, picnics, or any occasion where you want to enjoy the vibrant flavors of Mexican cuisine. Adjust the seasonings and toppings to suit your taste preferences, and get ready to savor the deliciousness of Elote!

Enchiladas Suizas

Ingredients:

For the Enchilada Filling:

- 2 cups cooked and shredded chicken (you can use rotisserie chicken)
- 1 small onion, finely chopped
- 2 cloves garlic, minced
- 1 tablespoon vegetable oil
- Salt and pepper to taste
- 1 teaspoon ground cumin
- 1 teaspoon chili powder
- 1/2 cup chopped fresh cilantro
- 1 cup shredded cheese (such as Monterey Jack or mozzarella)

For the Enchilada Sauce:

- 1 pound (about 500g) tomatillos, husks removed and rinsed
- 1 jalapeño pepper, stemmed and seeded
- 1/2 cup chopped onion
- 2 cloves garlic
- 1/4 cup chopped fresh cilantro
- 1 cup chicken broth
- 1/2 cup heavy cream
- Salt to taste

For Assembling and Serving:

- 12 corn tortillas
- 1 cup shredded cheese (for topping)
- Chopped fresh cilantro (for garnish)
- Sour cream (for serving, optional)

Instructions:

1. Preheat your oven to 375°F (190°C).

2. Make the Enchilada Filling:
   - In a skillet, heat the vegetable oil over medium heat. Add the chopped onion and minced garlic, and cook until softened and fragrant, about 3-4 minutes.
   - Add the shredded chicken to the skillet and season with salt, pepper, ground cumin, and chili powder. Cook for another 2-3 minutes until the chicken is heated through and well coated with the spices.
   - Stir in the chopped fresh cilantro and shredded cheese, and cook until the cheese is melted. Remove from heat and set aside.
3. Make the Enchilada Sauce:
   - In a blender or food processor, combine the tomatillos, jalapeño pepper, chopped onion, garlic cloves, and chopped cilantro. Blend until smooth.
   - Transfer the blended mixture to a saucepan. Add the chicken broth and bring to a simmer over medium heat. Let it simmer for about 5 minutes.
   - Stir in the heavy cream and season with salt to taste. Remove from heat and set aside.
4. Assemble the Enchiladas:
   - Warm the corn tortillas in the microwave or on a skillet until soft and pliable.
   - Place a spoonful of the chicken filling onto each tortilla and roll it up tightly. Place the rolled enchiladas seam side down in a baking dish.
5. Pour the Enchilada Sauce over the rolled enchiladas, covering them evenly.
6. Sprinkle the shredded cheese over the top of the enchiladas.
7. Bake the Enchiladas Suizas in the preheated oven for 20-25 minutes, or until the sauce is bubbly and the cheese is melted and golden brown.
8. Remove from the oven and garnish with chopped fresh cilantro.
9. Serve hot, with sour cream on the side if desired.
10. Enjoy your homemade Enchiladas Suizas, savoring the creamy sauce and flavorful filling!

Enchiladas Suizas make for a delicious and comforting meal that's perfect for family dinners or gatherings with friends. Adjust the level of spiciness by adding more or fewer jalapeño peppers to the sauce, and feel free to customize the filling with your favorite ingredients.

Carnitas Tacos

Ingredients:

For the Carnitas:

- 3 lbs (about 1.4 kg) boneless pork shoulder (also known as pork butt), trimmed of excess fat and cut into large chunks
- 1 onion, quartered
- 4 cloves garlic, smashed
- 2 bay leaves
- 1 teaspoon ground cumin
- 1 teaspoon dried oregano
- 1 teaspoon smoked paprika
- 1 teaspoon chili powder
- 1/2 teaspoon ground coriander
- Salt and pepper to taste
- 2 tablespoons vegetable oil

For Serving:

- Corn or flour tortillas
- Chopped onion
- Chopped cilantro
- Sliced radishes
- Lime wedges
- Salsa or hot sauce
- Sliced avocado or guacamole
- Crumbled cotija cheese or shredded cheese (optional)

Instructions:

1. Season the pork: In a large bowl, combine the pork chunks with the quartered onion, smashed garlic cloves, bay leaves, ground cumin, dried oregano, smoked paprika, chili powder, ground coriander, salt, and pepper. Toss until the pork is evenly coated with the seasoning mixture.

2. Slow-cook the pork: Heat the vegetable oil in a large Dutch oven or heavy-bottomed pot over medium-high heat. Once hot, add the seasoned pork chunks in a single layer, making sure not to overcrowd the pot. Brown the pork on all sides, working in batches if necessary. This step helps develop flavor.
3. Once the pork is browned, return all the pork to the pot. Add enough water to cover the pork halfway. Bring the liquid to a simmer, then reduce the heat to low. Cover the pot and let the pork simmer gently for about 2-3 hours, or until the pork is fork-tender and easily shreds apart.
4. Shred the pork: Once the pork is cooked, remove it from the pot and transfer it to a cutting board. Use two forks to shred the pork into bite-sized pieces.
5. Crisp the pork (optional): For extra flavor and texture, you can crisp up the shredded pork before serving. Heat a large skillet over medium-high heat and add a little oil. Add the shredded pork in batches, spreading it out in an even layer. Let it cook without stirring for a few minutes until it starts to brown and crisp up on the bottom. Then, flip the pork and let it crisp up on the other side.
6. Assemble the tacos: Warm the tortillas in a dry skillet or microwave until soft and pliable. Fill each tortilla with a generous portion of the shredded pork carnitas. Top with chopped onion, chopped cilantro, sliced radishes, and a squeeze of lime juice. Serve with salsa or hot sauce, sliced avocado or guacamole, and crumbled cotija cheese or shredded cheese if desired.
7. Enjoy your homemade carnitas tacos, savoring the tender and flavorful pork with all your favorite toppings!

Carnitas tacos are versatile and customizable, so feel free to adjust the toppings and seasonings according to your taste preferences. They're perfect for serving at parties, family dinners, or anytime you're craving authentic Mexican flavors.

Barbacoa Tacos

Ingredients:

For the Barbacoa:

- 3 lbs (about 1.4 kg) beef chuck roast or brisket, cut into large chunks
- 1 onion, chopped
- 4 cloves garlic, minced
- 2 chipotle peppers in adobo sauce, minced
- 2 tablespoons adobo sauce (from the canned chipotle peppers)
- 1/4 cup fresh lime juice
- 1/4 cup apple cider vinegar
- 1 tablespoon ground cumin
- 1 tablespoon dried oregano
- 1 teaspoon ground cloves
- 1 teaspoon ground cinnamon
- 1/2 cup beef broth
- Salt and pepper to taste
- 2 tablespoons vegetable oil

For Serving:

- Corn or flour tortillas
- Chopped onion
- Chopped cilantro
- Sliced radishes
- Lime wedges
- Salsa or hot sauce
- Sliced avocado or guacamole
- Crumbled cotija cheese or shredded cheese (optional)

Instructions:

1. Prepare the Barbacoa:

- In a blender or food processor, combine the chopped onion, minced garlic, chipotle peppers, adobo sauce, fresh lime juice, apple cider vinegar, ground cumin, dried oregano, ground cloves, ground cinnamon, beef broth, salt, and pepper. Blend until smooth.
- Place the beef chunks in a large bowl or resealable plastic bag. Pour the blended marinade over the beef, making sure it's evenly coated. Cover the bowl or seal the bag, and refrigerate for at least 4 hours, or preferably overnight, to allow the flavors to penetrate the meat.

2. Cook the Barbacoa:
    - Preheat your oven to 325°F (160°C).
    - Heat the vegetable oil in a large Dutch oven or heavy-bottomed pot over medium-high heat. Once hot, add the marinated beef chunks in a single layer, making sure not to overcrowd the pot. Brown the beef on all sides, working in batches if necessary.
    - Once all the beef is browned, return it to the pot. Pour any remaining marinade over the beef.
    - Cover the pot with a lid and transfer it to the preheated oven. Let the beef cook in the oven for about 3-4 hours, or until the meat is tender and easily shreds apart with a fork.
3. Assemble the Tacos:
    - Warm the tortillas in a dry skillet or microwave until soft and pliable.
    - Fill each tortilla with a generous portion of the cooked barbacoa beef.
    - Top the tacos with chopped onion, chopped cilantro, sliced radishes, and a squeeze of lime juice.
    - Serve with salsa or hot sauce, sliced avocado or guacamole, and crumbled cotija cheese or shredded cheese if desired.
4. Enjoy your homemade barbacoa tacos, savoring the tender and flavorful beef with all your favorite toppings!

Barbacoa tacos are perfect for serving at parties, family dinners, or anytime you're craving authentic Mexican flavors. Customize the toppings and seasonings to suit your taste preferences, and enjoy the deliciousness of homemade barbacoa tacos!

Al Pastor Tacos

Ingredients:

For the Al Pastor Marinade:

- 3 lbs (about 1.4 kg) boneless pork shoulder (also known as pork butt), thinly sliced or cut into thin strips
- 3 dried guajillo chilies, stemmed and seeded
- 3 dried ancho chilies, stemmed and seeded
- 3 cloves garlic, minced
- 1/2 cup chopped onion
- 1/4 cup white vinegar
- 1/4 cup pineapple juice
- 2 tablespoons achiote paste
- 1 tablespoon ground cumin
- 1 tablespoon dried oregano
- 1 teaspoon smoked paprika
- 1 teaspoon ground cinnamon
- Salt and pepper to taste

For Serving:

- Corn or flour tortillas
- Chopped pineapple
- Chopped onion
- Chopped cilantro
- Salsa or hot sauce
- Lime wedges

Instructions:

1. Prepare the Al Pastor Marinade:

- In a bowl, combine the dried guajillo chilies, dried ancho chilies, minced garlic, chopped onion, white vinegar, pineapple juice, achiote paste, ground cumin, dried oregano, smoked paprika, ground cinnamon, salt, and pepper.
- Use an immersion blender or regular blender to blend the ingredients until smooth, creating a thick marinade.

2. Marinate the Pork:
    - Place the thinly sliced or cut pork shoulder in a large bowl or resealable plastic bag.
    - Pour the Al Pastor marinade over the pork, making sure it's evenly coated. Cover the bowl or seal the bag, and refrigerate for at least 4 hours, or preferably overnight, to allow the flavors to penetrate the meat.
3. Cook the Al Pastor:
    - Preheat your grill or oven to medium-high heat.
    - If using a grill: Thread the marinated pork onto skewers, layering with pineapple chunks and onion slices. Grill the skewers, turning occasionally, until the pork is cooked through and caramelized, about 10-15 minutes.
    - If using an oven: Preheat the oven to 400°F (200°C). Spread the marinated pork in a single layer on a baking sheet lined with aluminum foil. Roast in the preheated oven for about 20-25 minutes, or until the pork is cooked through and caramelized, flipping halfway through.
4. Assemble the Tacos:
    - Warm the tortillas in a dry skillet or microwave until soft and pliable.
    - Fill each tortilla with a generous portion of the cooked Al Pastor pork.
    - Top the tacos with chopped pineapple, chopped onion, chopped cilantro, and a squeeze of lime juice.
    - Serve with salsa or hot sauce on the side.
5. Enjoy your homemade Al Pastor tacos, savoring the tender and flavorful pork with all your favorite toppings!

Al Pastor tacos are perfect for serving at parties, family dinners, or anytime you're craving authentic Mexican flavors. Customize the toppings and seasonings to suit your taste preferences, and enjoy the deliciousness of homemade Al Pastor tacos!

Pozole Rojo

Ingredients:

For the Pozole:

- 2 lbs (about 1 kg) pork shoulder, trimmed and cut into chunks
- 1 onion, quartered
- 4 cloves garlic, peeled and smashed
- 2 bay leaves
- 1 teaspoon dried oregano
- 1 teaspoon ground cumin
- 1 teaspoon salt, plus more to taste
- 1/2 teaspoon black pepper
- 6 cups chicken broth
- 2 cans (15 oz each) hominy, drained and rinsed

For the Red Chili Sauce:

- 4 dried guajillo chilies, stemmed and seeded
- 2 dried ancho chilies, stemmed and seeded
- 2 dried pasilla chilies, stemmed and seeded
- 2 cloves garlic, peeled
- 1/2 onion, chopped
- 1 teaspoon dried oregano
- 1 teaspoon ground cumin
- 1/2 teaspoon ground coriander
- 1/2 teaspoon ground cinnamon
- 4 cups water
- Salt to taste

For Serving:

- Shredded cabbage or lettuce
- Sliced radishes
- Chopped cilantro
- Lime wedges

- Sliced avocado
- Sliced jalapeños
- Corn tortillas or tostadas

Instructions:

1. Prepare the Pork:
    - In a large pot or Dutch oven, combine the pork shoulder chunks, quartered onion, smashed garlic cloves, bay leaves, dried oregano, ground cumin, salt, and black pepper.
    - Add the chicken broth to the pot, making sure the pork is fully submerged. Bring to a boil over high heat, then reduce the heat to low and let it simmer, partially covered, for about 1.5 to 2 hours, or until the pork is tender and easily shreds apart.
2. Prepare the Red Chili Sauce:
    - In a dry skillet over medium heat, lightly toast the dried guajillo, ancho, and pasilla chilies for about 1-2 minutes on each side until they become fragrant. Be careful not to burn them.
    - Transfer the toasted chilies to a bowl and cover them with hot water. Let them soak for about 20-30 minutes until they are softened.
    - In a blender, combine the soaked chilies (drained), garlic cloves, chopped onion, dried oregano, ground cumin, ground coriander, ground cinnamon, and water. Blend until smooth, adding more water if needed to achieve a pourable consistency. Season with salt to taste.
3. Finish the Pozole:
    - Once the pork is tender, remove the bay leaves and discard them. Remove the pork from the pot and shred it into bite-sized pieces using two forks.
    - Return the shredded pork to the pot.
    - Add the drained and rinsed hominy to the pot and stir to combine.
    - Pour the prepared red chili sauce into the pot and stir until the pork and hominy are coated.
    - Let the pozole simmer for an additional 15-20 minutes to allow the flavors to meld together. Adjust the seasoning with salt if needed.
4. Serve:
    - Ladle the pozole into bowls.
    - Serve with shredded cabbage or lettuce, sliced radishes, chopped cilantro, lime wedges, sliced avocado, sliced jalapeños, and warm corn tortillas or tostadas on the side.

- Enjoy your homemade Pozole Rojo, savoring its rich and comforting flavors!

Pozole Rojo is a hearty and satisfying dish that's perfect for serving at gatherings or for warming up on a cold day. Customize the toppings according to your taste preferences, and enjoy the deliciousness of this traditional Mexican soup!

Flan

Ingredients:

For the Caramel:

- 1 cup granulated sugar
- 1/4 cup water

For the Flan:

- 4 large eggs
- 1 can (14 oz) sweetened condensed milk
- 1 can (12 oz) evaporated milk
- 1 teaspoon vanilla extract

Instructions:

1. Preheat your oven to 350°F (175°C).
2. Prepare the Caramel:
   - In a small saucepan, combine the granulated sugar and water over medium heat.
   - Stir until the sugar has dissolved, then stop stirring and let the mixture simmer.
   - Cook the sugar mixture, swirling the pan occasionally, until it turns a deep amber color, about 10-12 minutes.
   - Quickly pour the caramel into the bottom of a 9-inch round cake pan or individual ramekins, swirling to evenly coat the bottom. Be careful as the caramel will be very hot. Set aside to cool and harden.
3. Prepare the Flan Custard:
   - In a large mixing bowl, whisk together the eggs, sweetened condensed milk, evaporated milk, and vanilla extract until well combined and smooth.
4. Pour the Flan Mixture:
   - Carefully pour the flan mixture over the cooled caramel layer in the cake pan or ramekins.

5. Bake the Flan:
   - Place the cake pan or ramekins in a larger baking dish or roasting pan. Fill the larger dish with hot water until it reaches halfway up the sides of the cake pan or ramekins, creating a water bath.
   - Carefully transfer the baking dish to the preheated oven.
   - Bake the flan for 45-50 minutes, or until the custard is set around the edges but still slightly jiggly in the center.
6. Chill and Serve:
   - Remove the flan from the oven and let it cool to room temperature.
   - Once cooled, cover the cake pan or ramekins with plastic wrap and refrigerate for at least 4 hours, or overnight, to chill and set completely.
7. Serve the Flan:
   - To serve, run a knife around the edges of the flan to loosen it from the sides of the pan or ramekins.
   - Place a serving plate upside down on top of the cake pan or ramekin and carefully invert the flan onto the plate. The caramel sauce will flow over the top.
   - Slice the flan into wedges if using a cake pan or serve each individual ramekin as is.
   - Enjoy your homemade flan chilled, savoring its creamy texture and sweet caramel flavor!

Flan is a delightful dessert that's perfect for serving at parties, special occasions, or any time you're craving a sweet treat. You can garnish it with whipped cream, fresh berries, or mint leaves for an extra touch of elegance.

Churros

Ingredients:

- 1 cup water
- 2 tablespoons white sugar
- 1/2 teaspoon salt
- 2 tablespoons vegetable oil
- 1 cup all-purpose flour
- Vegetable oil, for frying
- 1/2 cup white sugar
- 1 teaspoon ground cinnamon

For Serving:

- Chocolate sauce, dulce de leche, or caramel sauce (optional)

Instructions:

1. In a small saucepan, combine the water, 2 tablespoons of sugar, salt, and 2 tablespoons of vegetable oil. Bring the mixture to a boil over medium heat.
2. Remove the saucepan from the heat, and stir in the flour until the mixture forms a ball of dough. Let the dough cool slightly.
3. Heat vegetable oil in a deep fryer or large pot to 375°F (190°C).
4. While the oil is heating, mix together 1/2 cup of sugar and cinnamon in a shallow dish or bowl. Set aside.
5. Transfer the dough to a piping bag fitted with a star tip.
6. Once the oil is hot, pipe the dough directly into the hot oil, using scissors to cut the dough into 4-inch strips. Be careful not to overcrowd the frying pot.
7. Fry the churros until they are golden brown and crispy, about 2-3 minutes per side. Use tongs or a slotted spoon to remove them from the oil and transfer them to a paper towel-lined plate to drain.
8. While the churros are still warm, roll them in the cinnamon sugar mixture until they are evenly coated.
9. Serve the churros immediately, optionally with chocolate sauce, dulce de leche, or caramel sauce for dipping.

10. Enjoy your homemade churros as a delicious sweet treat!

Churros are best enjoyed fresh and warm, so serve them right away for the crispiest texture. They're perfect for breakfast, dessert, or anytime you're craving something sweet and comforting.

Sopapillas

Ingredients:

- 2 cups all-purpose flour
- 1 tablespoon baking powder
- 1/2 teaspoon salt
- 2 tablespoons granulated sugar
- 2 tablespoons vegetable oil or melted butter
- 2/3 cup warm water
- Vegetable oil, for frying
- Powdered sugar or cinnamon sugar, for dusting
- Honey or chocolate sauce, for drizzling (optional)

Instructions:

1. In a large mixing bowl, whisk together the all-purpose flour, baking powder, salt, and granulated sugar.
2. Add the vegetable oil or melted butter to the dry ingredients, and mix until crumbly.
3. Gradually add the warm water to the mixture, stirring until a dough forms. Knead the dough on a lightly floured surface until smooth and elastic, about 5 minutes.
4. Shape the dough into a ball, cover it with a clean kitchen towel, and let it rest for 15-20 minutes.
5. After the dough has rested, heat vegetable oil in a deep fryer or large pot to 375°F (190°C).
6. While the oil is heating, divide the dough into smaller portions and roll each portion out on a lightly floured surface to about 1/4 inch thickness.
7. Cut the rolled-out dough into squares or rectangles using a pizza cutter or knife.
8. Once the oil is hot, carefully fry the sopapillas in batches until they are puffed up and golden brown, flipping them once during cooking to ensure even browning. This typically takes about 1-2 minutes per side.
9. Use a slotted spoon or tongs to remove the fried sopapillas from the oil and transfer them to a paper towel-lined plate to drain excess oil.
10. While the sopapillas are still warm, dust them generously with powdered sugar or cinnamon sugar.

11. Serve the sopapillas immediately, optionally drizzling them with honey or chocolate sauce for extra sweetness.
12. Enjoy your homemade sopapillas as a delicious dessert or snack!

Sopapillas are best enjoyed warm and fresh, so serve them right away for the best texture and flavor. They're perfect for satisfying your sweet tooth and are sure to be a hit with family and friends!

Tres Leches Cake

Ingredients:

For the Cake:

- 1 cup all-purpose flour
- 1 1/2 teaspoons baking powder
- 1/4 teaspoon salt
- 5 large eggs, separated
- 1 cup granulated sugar, divided
- 1/3 cup whole milk
- 1 teaspoon vanilla extract

For the Three Milks Mixture:

- 1 can (12 oz) evaporated milk
- 1 can (14 oz) sweetened condensed milk
- 1 cup heavy cream

For the Topping:

- 2 cups whipped cream
- Maraschino cherries or fresh berries (for garnish, optional)

Instructions:

1. Preheat your oven to 350°F (175°C). Grease and flour a 9x13-inch baking dish.
2. In a medium bowl, sift together the all-purpose flour, baking powder, and salt. Set aside.
3. In a large mixing bowl, beat the egg yolks with 3/4 cup of granulated sugar until pale and fluffy. Stir in the whole milk and vanilla extract.
4. Gradually add the dry ingredients to the egg yolk mixture, stirring until well combined.

5. In a separate clean mixing bowl, beat the egg whites until soft peaks form. Gradually add the remaining 1/4 cup of granulated sugar and continue beating until stiff peaks form.
6. Gently fold the beaten egg whites into the cake batter until just combined, being careful not to deflate the mixture.
7. Pour the batter into the prepared baking dish and spread it out evenly.
8. Bake the cake in the preheated oven for 25-30 minutes, or until a toothpick inserted into the center comes out clean and the top is golden brown.
9. While the cake is baking, prepare the three milks mixture by combining the evaporated milk, sweetened condensed milk, and heavy cream in a bowl. Stir until well combined.
10. Once the cake is baked, remove it from the oven and let it cool slightly in the baking dish for about 10 minutes.
11. Using a fork or skewer, poke holes all over the surface of the warm cake.
12. Slowly pour the three milks mixture over the warm cake, making sure to evenly soak it. Allow the cake to absorb the mixture for at least 30 minutes, or refrigerate overnight for best results.
13. Once the cake has soaked up the three milks mixture, spread whipped cream over the top.
14. Garnish the Tres Leches Cake with maraschino cherries or fresh berries, if desired.
15. Slice and serve the Tres Leches Cake chilled, savoring its rich and creamy texture!

Tres Leches Cake is a delightful dessert that's perfect for celebrations, gatherings, or anytime you're craving something sweet and indulgent. Enjoy the deliciousness of this classic Latin American treat!

Mexican Wedding Cookies

Ingredients:

- 1 cup (2 sticks) unsalted butter, softened
- 1/2 cup powdered sugar, plus more for coating
- 1 teaspoon vanilla extract
- 2 cups all-purpose flour
- 1 cup finely chopped nuts (such as pecans or walnuts)

Instructions:

1. Preheat your oven to 350°F (175°C). Line a baking sheet with parchment paper or silicone baking mat.
2. In a large mixing bowl, cream together the softened butter and 1/2 cup of powdered sugar until light and fluffy.
3. Add the vanilla extract to the butter-sugar mixture and mix until well combined.
4. Gradually add the all-purpose flour to the mixture, mixing until a dough forms.
5. Stir in the finely chopped nuts until evenly distributed throughout the dough.
6. Shape the dough into 1-inch balls and place them on the prepared baking sheet, spacing them about 1 inch apart.
7. Bake the cookies in the preheated oven for 10-12 minutes, or until set but not browned.
8. Remove the cookies from the oven and let them cool on the baking sheet for a few minutes.
9. While the cookies are still warm, roll them in powdered sugar to coat evenly. You can also gently shake off any excess powdered sugar.
10. Transfer the coated cookies to a wire rack to cool completely.
11. Once cooled, roll the cookies in powdered sugar again to ensure they are fully coated.
12. Store the Mexican Wedding Cookies in an airtight container at room temperature for up to one week.
13. Serve and enjoy these delicious, buttery cookies as a sweet treat for weddings, holidays, or any occasion!

Mexican Wedding Cookies are perfect for gifting, sharing, or enjoying with a cup of coffee or tea. They melt in your mouth and have a delightful nutty flavor that makes them irresistible!

Margaritas

Ingredients:

- 2 oz (60 ml) tequila
- 1 oz (30 ml) lime juice, freshly squeezed
- 1/2 oz (15 ml) orange liqueur (triple sec or Cointreau)
- 1/2 oz (15 ml) simple syrup or agave nectar
- Ice
- Salt, for rimming the glass (optional)
- Lime wedges, for garnish

Instructions:

1. Rim the glass: If desired, prepare the glass by rubbing a lime wedge around the rim to moisten it, then dip the rim into a plate of salt to coat it.
2. Fill a cocktail shaker with ice.
3. Add the tequila, freshly squeezed lime juice, orange liqueur, and simple syrup or agave nectar to the shaker.
4. Shake the ingredients well until the shaker is frosty on the outside.
5. Strain the Margarita mixture into the prepared glass filled with fresh ice.
6. Garnish with a lime wedge on the rim of the glass.
7. Serve and enjoy your homemade Margarita!

Variations:

- Frozen Margarita: Blend the Margarita ingredients with ice until smooth and slushy.
- Flavored Margarita: Add fruit puree (such as strawberry, mango, or pineapple) to the Margarita mixture for a fruity twist.
- Spicy Margarita: Add a slice of jalapeño or a dash of hot sauce to the Margarita mixture for a spicy kick.
- Skinny Margarita: Use fresh lime juice and agave nectar instead of simple syrup to reduce the calorie content.

Margaritas are perfect for sipping on a warm day, at parties, or alongside Mexican cuisine. Adjust the proportions of ingredients to suit your taste preferences, and enjoy this refreshing and iconic cocktail! Remember to drink responsibly.

Horchata

Ingredients:

- 1 cup long-grain white rice
- 4 cups water, plus more for soaking
- 1 cinnamon stick
- 1/2 cup granulated sugar, or to taste
- 1 teaspoon vanilla extract
- Ground cinnamon, for garnish (optional)

Instructions:

1. Rinse the rice: Place the white rice in a fine-mesh strainer and rinse it thoroughly under cold water until the water runs clear. This helps remove excess starch from the rice.
2. Soak the rice: Transfer the rinsed rice to a large bowl and cover it with water. Let the rice soak for at least 4 hours or overnight. Soaking the rice helps soften it and makes it easier to blend.
3. Blend the rice mixture: After soaking, drain the rice and discard the soaking water. Transfer the soaked rice to a blender. Add 4 cups of fresh water and the cinnamon stick to the blender. Blend on high speed for 1-2 minutes, or until the rice is finely ground and the mixture is smooth.
4. Strain the mixture: Place a fine-mesh strainer or cheesecloth over a large bowl or pitcher. Pour the blended rice mixture through the strainer, pressing down with a spoon to extract as much liquid as possible. Discard the solids left in the strainer.
5. Sweeten and flavor the Horchata: Stir in the granulated sugar and vanilla extract into the strained rice milk mixture until the sugar is dissolved. Adjust the sweetness and flavor to your taste preferences, adding more sugar or vanilla if desired.
6. Chill the Horchata: Cover the pitcher or bowl containing the Horchata with plastic wrap or a lid and refrigerate it for at least 1-2 hours, or until thoroughly chilled. Chilling the Horchata allows the flavors to meld together.
7. Serve the Horchata: Stir the Horchata well before serving. Pour it into glasses filled with ice cubes. Optionally, sprinkle ground cinnamon on top for garnish.
8. Enjoy your homemade Horchata! Sip and savor the creamy, cinnamon-infused flavor of this refreshing beverage.

Horchata is best enjoyed fresh and chilled. It's a delightful drink to serve at parties, gatherings, or alongside your favorite Mexican dishes. Adjust the sweetness and flavor to suit your preferences, and enjoy the cool and creamy goodness of homemade Horchata!

Micheladas

Ingredients:

- 1 lime wedge, for rimming the glass
- Salt or Tajín seasoning, for rimming the glass (optional)
- Ice
- 1 (12 oz) bottle of Mexican lager beer (such as Modelo, Tecate, or Corona)
- 2 tablespoons lime juice, freshly squeezed
- 1 teaspoon hot sauce (such as Tabasco or Cholula), or to taste
- 1 teaspoon Worcestershire sauce
- 1/2 teaspoon soy sauce
- Pinch of ground black pepper
- Pinch of ground cayenne pepper or chili powder
- Tajín seasoning or additional lime wedges, for garnish (optional)

Instructions:

1. Rim the glass: Run a lime wedge around the rim of a glass to moisten it. Dip the moistened rim into a plate of salt or Tajín seasoning to coat it evenly. Set aside.
2. Fill the glass with ice cubes.
3. Squeeze the lime juice: Squeeze the juice of one lime wedge into the glass over the ice.
4. Add the sauces and seasonings: Pour in the hot sauce, Worcestershire sauce, soy sauce, ground black pepper, and ground cayenne pepper or chili powder into the glass.
5. Mix the ingredients: Use a spoon or stir stick to mix the ingredients well, ensuring they are evenly distributed.
6. Pour the beer: Slowly pour the Mexican lager beer into the glass over the ice and seasoned mixture. Leave room at the top to prevent overflow.
7. Garnish the Michelada: Optionally, garnish the Michelada with a sprinkle of Tajín seasoning or an additional lime wedge on the rim of the glass for extra flavor and presentation.
8. Serve and enjoy your homemade Michelada! Sip and savor the refreshing and savory flavors of this classic Mexican cocktail.

Micheladas are perfect for enjoying on a hot day, at parties, or alongside your favorite Mexican dishes. Adjust the ingredients to suit your taste preferences, adding more or less hot sauce and seasonings as desired. Remember to drink responsibly!

Agua Fresca

Ingredients:

- 4 cups chopped fresh fruit (such as watermelon, cantaloupe, strawberries, mango, pineapple, cucumber, or a combination)
- 4 cups water
- 1/4 cup granulated sugar, honey, or agave nectar (adjust to taste)
- Juice of 1-2 limes or lemons (optional, for added brightness)

Instructions:

1. Prepare the fruit: Wash and chop the fresh fruit into small pieces. Remove any seeds or pits as needed.
2. Blend the fruit: In a blender, combine the chopped fruit with 2 cups of water. Blend on high speed until the fruit is pureed and smooth.
3. Strain the mixture: Place a fine-mesh strainer or cheesecloth over a large bowl or pitcher. Pour the blended fruit mixture through the strainer, pressing down with a spoon to extract as much liquid as possible. Discard the solids left in the strainer.
4. Sweeten the Agua Fresca: Stir in the granulated sugar, honey, or agave nectar into the strained fruit juice until it's fully dissolved. Adjust the sweetness to your taste preferences, adding more sweetener if desired.
5. Dilute with water: Add the remaining 2 cups of water to the sweetened fruit juice and stir until well combined. You can adjust the amount of water based on your desired consistency—add more for a lighter drink or less for a more concentrated flavor.
6. Add citrus juice (optional): Squeeze the juice of 1-2 limes or lemons into the Agua Fresca for added brightness and acidity. Stir well to incorporate.
7. Chill the Agua Fresca: Cover the pitcher or bowl containing the Agua Fresca with plastic wrap or a lid and refrigerate it for at least 1-2 hours, or until thoroughly chilled. Chilling the Agua Fresca allows the flavors to meld together.
8. Serve the Agua Fresca: Stir the Agua Fresca well before serving. Pour it into glasses filled with ice cubes.
9. Garnish (optional): Garnish each glass with a slice of fruit or a sprig of mint for a decorative touch.
10. Enjoy your homemade Agua Fresca! Sip and savor the refreshing and fruity flavors of this delightful beverage.

Agua Fresca is a versatile drink that can be made with a variety of fruits, making it perfect for using up seasonal produce or experimenting with different flavor combinations. It's a great alternative to sugary sodas and juices, and it's sure to be a hit with family and friends, especially on hot summer days!

Paloma

Ingredients:

- 2 oz (60 ml) tequila
- 1/2 oz (15 ml) lime juice, freshly squeezed
- 4 oz (120 ml) grapefruit soda (such as Jarritos or Squirt)
- Splash of soda water
- Lime wedge, for garnish
- Salt or Tajín seasoning, for rimming the glass (optional)

Instructions:

1. Rim the glass: Run a lime wedge around the rim of a glass to moisten it. Dip the moistened rim into a plate of salt or Tajín seasoning to coat it evenly. Set aside.
2. Fill the glass with ice cubes.
3. Add the tequila and freshly squeezed lime juice to the glass.
4. Pour the grapefruit soda into the glass over the tequila and lime juice.
5. Top off the drink with a splash of soda water for a bit of effervescence.
6. Stir gently to combine the ingredients.
7. Garnish the Paloma with a lime wedge on the rim of the glass.
8. Serve and enjoy your homemade Paloma! Sip and savor the refreshing and citrusy flavors of this classic Mexican cocktail.

Variations:

- Spicy Paloma: Add a slice of jalapeño or a dash of hot sauce to the Paloma for a spicy kick.
- Paloma de Pepino: Add cucumber slices to the Paloma for a refreshing twist.
- Skinny Paloma: Use fresh grapefruit juice and agave nectar instead of grapefruit soda for a lighter version of the cocktail.

The Paloma is a versatile and customizable cocktail that's perfect for enjoying on any occasion. Adjust the proportions of ingredients to suit your taste preferences, and remember to drink responsibly!

Mexican Hot Chocolate

Ingredients:

- 3 cups whole milk
- 4 oz (about 120g) Mexican chocolate or bittersweet chocolate, chopped
- 2 tablespoons granulated sugar, or to taste
- 1 teaspoon ground cinnamon
- 1/4 teaspoon ground nutmeg (optional)
- Pinch of cayenne pepper or chili powder (optional, for added heat)
- Whipped cream, marshmallows, or cinnamon sticks, for serving (optional)

Instructions:

1. In a saucepan, heat the whole milk over medium heat until it starts to steam, but do not let it boil.
2. Add the chopped Mexican chocolate or bittersweet chocolate to the warm milk. Stir continuously until the chocolate is completely melted and the mixture is smooth and creamy.
3. Stir in the granulated sugar, ground cinnamon, and ground nutmeg (if using) until the sugar is dissolved and the spices are evenly distributed.
4. For a spicy kick, add a pinch of cayenne pepper or chili powder to the hot chocolate mixture. Adjust the amount according to your taste preferences.
5. Once everything is well combined and heated through, remove the saucepan from the heat.
6. Pour the Mexican Hot Chocolate into mugs or cups.
7. Serve the Mexican Hot Chocolate hot, optionally topped with whipped cream, marshmallows, or a cinnamon stick for garnish.
8. Enjoy your homemade Mexican Hot Chocolate! Sip and savor the rich and indulgent flavors of this comforting beverage.

Variations:

- Vegan Mexican Hot Chocolate: Use non-dairy milk (such as almond milk or coconut milk) and dairy-free chocolate to make a vegan version of this drink.

- Mocha Mexican Hot Chocolate: Add a shot of espresso or strongly brewed coffee to the hot chocolate mixture for a caffeinated twist.
- Mexican Hot Chocolate with Rum: Add a splash of rum or spiced rum to the hot chocolate for a boozy variation.

Mexican Hot Chocolate is perfect for warming up on chilly days or for indulging in a cozy evening at home. Customize the spices and sweetness level to suit your taste preferences, and enjoy this classic and comforting drink!

www.ingramcontent.com/pod-product-compliance
Lightning Source LLC
LaVergne TN
LVHW081600060526
838201LV00054B/1999